SpringerBriefs in Economics

More information about this series at http://www.springer.com/series/8876

Stuart Birks

Rethinking Economics

From Analogies to the Real World

Springer

Stuart Birks
Massey University
Palmerston North
New Zealand

ISSN 2191-5504 ISSN 2191-5512 (electronic)
ISBN 978-981-287-175-6 ISBN 978-981-287-176-3 (eBook)
DOI 10.1007/978-981-287-176-3

Library of Congress Control Number: 2014946772

Springer Singapore Heidelberg New York Dordrecht London

Printed on acid-free paper

Springer is part of Springer Science+Business Media (www.springer.com)

Preface

My initial economics training at Essex University and the London School of Economics over 40 years ago focused on mathematical economics and econometrics. This was unusual for the time, it being a time when there was more emphasis on descriptive and historical analyses and many years before the existence of PCs, the internet and online databases. I followed that with a period in strategic planning, working in a multidisciplinary context and considering real-world policy problems. This cross-disciplinary applied work proved invaluable in shaping my perspective on the application of economics. I was interested to find that the questions addressed were very different from the questions that I had seen set up and readily answered with the techniques and models that I had been taught. This suggested that maybe economists were setting problems for reasons other than relevance. A mathematical model could be used to solve a particular problem. It could identify the maximum quantity of a homogeneous good that could be produced with a given, mathematically appropriate (differentiable, etc.) production function and (linear) cost constraint. Returns to education could be identified by considering earnings differences by qualification for people at different ages (although there are other benefits to education and current pay differentials by age may not be sustained in the future). The focus was on those sorts of problems rather than looking at the policy issues that may be of greatest importance at that time. It might also mean that policy issues were, and still are, framed in a way that best suits the models, rather than the approaches that are most relevant for those particular issues.[1]

I then returned to academia, spending many years working in areas of land economics, public sector economics, health, education and social issues. This included participation in and presentation at conferences for politics, health,

[1] More suitable approaches may include cross-disciplinary work as with an education project assessing policy proposals that used econometrics in an attempt to improve the quality of teaching in schools (Birks et al. 2013; Snook et al. 2013). Economics can only be applied in an area if the analysis includes relevant information on that area of application, be it health, education, agriculture, the environment, or whatever. There are few, if any, purely economic policy issues.

communication, law and many other areas. In contrast, economics conferences seemed to be inward looking, bounded by the constraints of the discipline as it had evolved. Even so, the various academic and practitioner groups in the other conferences had their own perspectives and understanding of issues. Where there was limited communication across groups, the members of a group frequently came to see their own perceptions as representing knowledge of the world, often of a nature not available to the uninitiated. Once I had observed what appeared to be flawed or unduly rigid reasoning by those of other disciplines, I realised that the same points could be made about economists. It is often easier to see things when somewhat detached from the situation that when immersed in it. It is for this reason that there are examples in this book that I have taken from areas outside economics.

I learned another lesson from my continued exposure to cross-disciplinary audiences in relation to both research and teaching. It led me to see that strong points could be made without requiring detailed technical exposition. This is important if the points are to be accessible to a wide audience. It reflects the ways in which I modified my courses to provide something that I felt was more palatable than equations and symbols. I also realised that it is important to understand the context in which economics is applied if the economics input is to be relevant.

Much of this context is actually missing in standard economic theory because these aspects are assumed away. When learning the economic theories and methods, there is generally no specific application in mind, and therefore some general representation, such as of the firm and the consumers, it used as the starting point. This context has shaped the structures that are available to be applied in specific instances.

I also noticed major issues in terms of the quantitative analyses used in relation to economics. In particular, I found when teaching econometrics that more and more of my time was spent on the issues leading up to the development of the model, such as the data, the relationships and the phenomena under investigation. These can shape the sort of representations that are required and the interpretation of results afterwards. This is very different from the standard emphasis on technical, statistical problems such as heteroskedasticity, multicollinearity, autocorrelation and unit roots. These are the standard problems that econometricians look for in terms of critiquing econometric studies, but there are many other things that are very important.

Over the years, people have said to me that I should put this material together into a book. Responding to this challenge, I have compiled here, out of a lot of material, a condensed selection presenting some of the main points. I think attention spans these days are getting shorter. Even courses are getting shorter, and so what is needed is some brief, clear representation of some key points. Some economists may choose to select from these to critique the approaches they are taking. Perhaps it will lead them to modify the sort of analysis that they do. It may also help them and others, including non-economists, to critically interpret analyses that others have done. Hopefully, I have something that is relatively concise and clear and useful to some with interest in these areas.

While some might see this as a critique of economics, I would rather think of it as indicating how, with care, much can be taken from the existing body economics knowledge. If these limitations are recognised, along with the additional reserves, qualifications and adjustments that are needed, a lot can be usefully applied to give an improved understanding of the world. The direction may not be self-evident to those who see progress in terms of greater sophistication of analysis. However, it does fit the perspective of those who are concerned that, to quote from an American Economic Association presidential address, "the mainstream of economic theory sacrifices far too much relevance in its insistent pursuit of ever increasing rigor" (Gordon 1976, p. 1).

Having taught economic principles from a highly critical perspective, it has become clear to me that this is by no means a negative exercise. Instead, it shows that there is much for debate and development. It is potentially a very interesting and exciting area. It is possible to break free from the constraints of a tight theoretical perspective, and see how the tools of economics can be used to address more grounded real-world issues. This involves a recognition of the strengths and weaknesses of the tools, and the limitations of the different perspectives. Other material can then be incorporated to broaden out the whole nature of the analysis. This suggests that economists potentially face a very exciting time in which a great deal of innovation is possible. The current state of knowledge provides some insights, but there are many things that need to be taken into account more effectively than at present. There are many challenges to be faced moving forward and developing a more grounded understanding of the economy and society.

The title of this book begins with the words, 'Rethinking Economics'. I used it first for a series of Economics Papers while on sabbatical at Bristol Business School in 2012, but I lay no claim to the term. It has been used by Kurien (1996), and has subsequently been adopted by a community of students and others who have been voicing their dissatisfaction with the narrow methodological and theoretical focus of economics as it is currently taught in universities. They are, "organising to create fresh economic narratives to challenge and enrich the predominant neoclassical narrative".[2] Another indication of this dissatisfaction is the rapid growth of the World Economics Association,[3] a global pluralist group with over 12,000 members. It supports, "the free exploration of economic reality from any perspective that adds to the sum of our understanding". These and other organisations around the world are questioning some of the dominant ideas in economics today, and trying to encourage more diverse and innovative approaches. It is hoped that this book contributes in some small way to those initiatives.

Palmerston North
New Zealand, June 2014

Stuart Birks

---

[2] http://www.rethinkecon.co.uk/.

[3] http://www.worldeconomicsassociation.org/.

References

Birks S, Snook I, Prochnow J, Rawlins P, O'Neill J (2013) Econometrics for education policy CPPE Issues Paper Series (Vol. 16). Palmerston North, Centre for Public Policy Evaluation, Massey University

Gordon RA (1976) Rigor and relevance in a changing institutional setting. Am Econ Rev 66(1): 1–14. doi: 10.2307/1804941

Kurien CT (1996) Rethinking economics: reflections based on a study of the Indian economy. Sage Publications, New Delhi

Snook I, O'Neill J, Birks S, Church J, Rawlins P (2013) The assessment of teacher quality: An investigation into current issues in evaluating and rewarding teachers. New Zealand, Education Policy Response Group, Institute of Education, Massey University, p 1–119

Acknowledgments

This book is the product of work over many years, and has benefited from my exposure to a wide range of academic and policy environments. I am indebted to the academic staff at the University of Essex and the London School of Economics many years ago for emphasising the importance of high intellectual standards while also giving the freedom to challenge established ideas. I hope that I have not let them down. My time outside academia gave invaluable experience of cross-disciplinary teamwork and insights into policy making and implementation. I am also grateful for the encouragement and advice of many of my more recent academic colleagues, especially in regard to this particular work. Any listing of names is problematic, but I am indebted in various ways to Mary Hedges, the late Gary Buurman, Jim Alvey, Neil Campbell, Srikanta Chatterjee, Allan Rae, Bryce Wilkinson, John Creedy and C.T. Kurien. Particular mention should also go to Frank Stilwell and others in the Sydney economics community for providing a lively, stimulating environment. Economics staff at the University of the West of England also made me very welcome while much of this material was refined. Of these, I am particularly grateful to Don Webber, whose enthusiasm and advice has been invaluable. Last but not least, Edward Fullbrook and others in the World Economics Association have enabled me to feel part of a broad, global community committed to ensuring that economics is relevant for the real world.

Contents

Chapter 1
The Importance of Rhetoric and Framing

Abstract People describe phenomena in an attempt to understand them and to persuade others to accept some preferred position. Rhetoric relates to persuasion, and framing refers to the process of description through selection, emphasis, exclusion and elaboration. Economists focus on theory and empirical analysis. There are aspects of rhetoric and framing in this process. This chapter outlines the nature and importance of this. It identifies three paths which have received relatively little attention. The paths are from theory to the real world, from theory to empirical analysis and from empirical results to the real world. They have important implications for policy making.

Keywords Rhetoric · Framing · Agenda setting · Traction · Paradigm · Analogy

I recall early in my time as an economist hearing the claim that it does not matter if economics does not describe the real world. It is enough that people are being taught 'to think like economists'. By this is meant that there is value in 'the economic way of thinking', perhaps in reference to an unspecified but assumed systematic, structured and logical approach to analysis. So what does it really mean? Is this 'way of thinking' of some intrinsic value, and can it be safely applied in general if the specific application as presented is questionable?

There is one approach which has come to dominate economics teaching. It is now referred to as 'mainstream economics', a term which is often taken as synonymous with neoclassical economics. Heterodox and pluralist economists present alternative perspectives. Using the concept of paradigms, the issue can be framed in terms of a 'mainstream paradigm' and the need for some alternative(s). Pluralism emphasises the co-existence of alternatives, and the debate is largely constrained to lie within the 'set of alternative paradigms'. Pluralist economics courses commonly cover a number of these options, suggesting a choice from Neoclassical, Post Keynesian, Marxist, Institutional, Austrian, Behavioural and other alternatives (Chang 2014, in his Chap. 4, outlines nine different schools). There are also an increasing number of critiques of mainstream economics, some of which are mentioned in Sect. 2.2. There is already an extensive and growing literature on these themes, but they are not the main focus of this book. Instead, it considers other, less well-recognised issues.

S. Birks, *Rethinking Economics*, SpringerBriefs in Economics,
DOI 10.1007/978-981-287-176-3_1

There are aspects which are commonly downplayed or overlooked by economists. The use of theory to understand real-world phenomena can be considered according to the framing described in Sect. 1.1. There I suggest that there are aspects of the application of theory which merit particular attention. Three areas of potential error are highlighted. They relate to three paths: (i) the link between theory and the real world, (ii) the relationship between theory and empirical analysis and (iii) the application of empirical results in decision making and implementation. This is followed in Sect. 1.2.1 by a brief discussion on rhetoric. It is important that economists have some awareness of the literature on rhetoric, if only the most basic of outlines, given that many textbooks still present the oversimplified distinction between positive and normative statements. The first of the three paths is discussed in the next chapter, with questions being raised about the nature and role of theories, and the possible misuse of theory. This is followed by chapters on the second and third paths. A closing chapter discusses possible future directions.

1.1 Three Paths

Let us step back and consider the broad approach taken by economists in their efforts to expound the discipline. In a discussion on the structure of argumentation in economics, Klamer refers to gaps in the reasoning:

> Gaps between the theoretical and empirical arguments have not been bridged, policy implications do not necessarily follow and methodological arguments are, for the most part, seriously flawed. (Klamer 2007, p. 106)

I have constructed Fig. 1.1 to make broadly similar points, focusing on the application of points to real-world decisions. It highlights three areas which, I suggest, have received too little attention.[1] In particular, the arrows in the diagram are intended to highlight potential difficulties in the translation of results from one area of analysis to another as described by paths A, B and C. In these moves across areas unrecognised errors are likely to arise. The diagram could be modified to include feedback from the real world impacting on theory and empirical analysis, or from empirical analysis to theory where findings appear to be inconsistent with a theory. This raises further issues about the political and institutional environment in which theories and techniques evolve. They are important, and feedbacks will

[1] The diagram highlights another possible concern, as highlighted by one commentator. The separation of theory and empirical analysis, combined with the nature of journal publication, may have led to a heavy emphasis on empirical analyses and a corresponding lack of attention to theoretical issues.

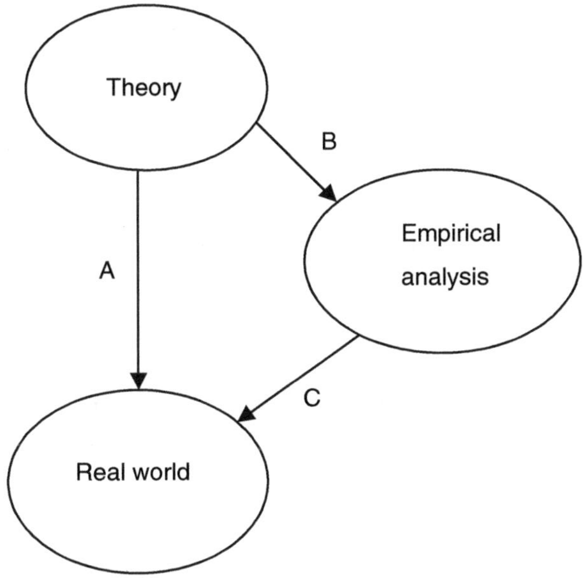

Fig. 1.1 Logical errors, types *A*, *B* and *C*

occur. However, as discussed in Chap. 2, there may be barriers to change when this involves challenges to established positions.[2]

Any theory should be internally logically consistent. Similarly, empirical analysis should be based on sound methodology. However, these two requirements are not sufficient for the use of these approaches to be meaningful for real-world issues. There are problems with A, B and C. Theoretical findings, being based on specific assumptions, may not translate directly to the real world (path A). The relationships or theoretical findings may also not be accurately or uniquely described in empirical formulations (path B). The results of empirical analyses may not support the claims made about their real-world implications (path C). In each of these cases, the paths may not be based on logic, in which case they rely on rhetoric. People, often unaware, are prepared to accept flawed reasoning. Consequently, these three types of error are highlighted through this structure. They form the basis for the following three chapters.

To see the point of the diagram, note that economists have put a lot of effort into the development of theory, requiring tight specification and internal consistency, and into empirical analysis, primarily econometrics, considering appropriate estimation methods and statistical tests suitable for hypothesis testing, for example. It is to be hoped that any theory is internally logically consistent. Similarly, empirical

[2] Peer review and research assessment exercises tend to constrain research to lie within the bounds of Kuhn's 'normal science', where the fundamentals are not challenged. A few key institutions, organisations and journals can be very influential in defining what is 'acceptable' (Gillies 2006). Chang (2014) describes some of these constraints when he writes of mainstream economics being defined by its theoretical approach rather than its subject matter.

analysis should be based on sound methodology. However, these two requirements, as contained within the ovals in the diagram, are not sufficient for the use of these approaches to be meaningful for real-world issues. Nevertheless, conclusions are commonly drawn on the basis of accepted conventions for the application of standard techniques and interpretation of results.

Mainstream theoretical approaches have been criticised (Dow 2012; Lawson 1997, 2003), as have the statistical approaches, especially in relation to hypothesis testing and the fallacy of the transposed conditional (McCloskey 1998; Ziliak and McCloskey 2008). However, less attention has been given to paths A, B and C. Each of these can be a source of error in understanding the real world. The points raised are not unique to the practice of mainstream economics. Similar points could be raised with alternative theoretical perspectives and empirical analyses that attempt to explain the real world. It is the extra aspects, the pieces that are omitted, that must later be added in or refined to get a clearer understanding.

Note that the diagram focuses on flows of information from analysis to real-world application. There are likely to be flows in the reverse direction also, but my concern here is in the use of economics in decision making, hence the limitation. The paths can be described as follows:

Type-A errors arise when theoretical results are assumed to be directly applicable to the real world.

Type-B errors arise when empirical formulations do not accurately reflect the underlying theory. This can be due to data problems, or difficulties specifying relationships and functional forms that match the theory.

Type-C errors occur when incorrect conclusions are drawn from statistical results, either through a misinterpretation of the meaning of the results, or a failure to consider additional, relevant policy dimensions.

This is the framing that I have chosen to present my points and, hopefully, persuade readers of their relevance. Consequently I am using it for rhetorical purposes. Concepts of rhetoric and framing are not widely used by economists. They are central to my story,[3] however, so the following section gives a short outline and discussion of them.

[3] We are all story tellers, even when the stories are dressed up with equations, tables and graphs. An underlying theme of this book is that the development of ideas, the provision of information, the choice of conclusions and the significance of those conclusions are developed in a political environment. The politics in relation to academia, the political sphere, and the news media is very important in terms of its implications for public perceptions of issues. It shapes what is considered acceptable and what is considered correct. There is a heavy subjective dimension to people's willingness to agree or disagree with findings presented to them, and also to the conclusions that researchers are prepared to draw from their analyses. These aspects also need to be understood in order to judge the value of findings and to understand the environment in which findings are used.

1.2 Rhetoric and Framing

As might be expected, rhetoric is used by all sides in debate. Rhetoric is about persuasion, and debates consist of people attempting to persuade others (and perhaps themselves) to see things in their preferred way.

Economists have been widely criticised for their unrealistic representations of the real world. 'Soundbites' can be useful rhetorical devices. One to note is, 'the map is not the territory' (Kay 2011). Simplified representations of phenomena do not equate to the phenomena themselves. Economic models are not the economy.

Recognition by others of rhetoric in economics extends to the extreme point where economics itself has been described as being little more than a rhetorical device. Its purpose is to persuade people to accept some preferred policy positions (Dunn 2004). Dunn is writing about the processes of policy making. He suggests that the use of complex models and involved statistical techniques can suppress criticism and sway an audience. Claims can be made that are hard to challenge without the relevant underlying knowledge. It is partly in response to this that the current book has been written. Some of the complexities can be explained in easily understood terms, as can the limitations of the techniques.

While rhetoric and persuasion convey a sense of intent, a more neutral, but equally important concept is that of 'framing'. The way an issue is presented affects what is seen and not seen, how it is understood and the conclusions drawn. Any analysis involves framing. It is an essential aspect of structured assessment. This has to be understood in a careful reflection on the nature of understanding. For example, a representation of a market by means of supply and demand curves assumes a homogeneous product, emphasises price as central to competition and market adjustment, and is based on static analysis rather than a series of events through time.

How can we limit the misinformation that might arise from a chosen framing? Keynes recognised the problem. As described later in this book, he was aware of the need to revisit the premises on which economic theory is based and to attend to additional reserves, qualifications and adjustments when applying findings from mathematical economics, too much of which are:

> …merely concoctions, as imprecise as the initial assumptions they rest on, which allow the author to lose sight of the complexities and interdependencies of the real world in a maze of pretentious and unhelpful symbols. (Keynes 2007, p. 298)

Commonly raised points of concern include assumptions of exogenous preferences and rational behaviour. Disregard for processes of deliberation and political decision making have also drawn critical comment from elsewhere. Much of this criticism is directed at what might be termed 'mainstream' economics. However, the issues are broader than this. Many of the points raised in the following chapters have relevance for economics in general and for wider academic discourse.

1.2.1 Rhetoric

So what is rhetoric? As a first step, it is important to be able to distinguish between logic, with its focus on proof, and rhetoric, relating to persuasion. If people were purely logical, there would not be a distinct area of study called rhetoric. People would only be persuaded by logical argument. This is not the case, with persuasion by other means often succeeding over a logical argument. Rhetoric is unlikely to have even developed as a separate field of study if people were only persuaded by logical arguments. Going back in time, study of rhetoric can be traced back at least to the fourth century BC (Aristotle 1954). It was addressed by Smith (1963) in a series of lectures in the 1760s, by which time rhetoric had been long established as a major component of the curriculum. Among other things, Smith referred to deliberative eloquence and judicial eloquence, these being the use of rhetoric in politics and in law, respectively.[4] Schopenhauer (1851) presented 38 stratagems for winning arguments. Stratagem No.28 makes the point that a logic-based response to rhetorical criticism would not be effective. Such a defence, 'would require a long explanation…and a reference to the principles of the branch of knowledge in question, or to the elements of the matter which you are discussing; and people are not disposed to listen to it'.

McCloskey (1998) has contended that economics has its own rhetoric, with support being given by others including Klamer (2007). Rhetoric is based on persuading a particular audience, and the rhetoric of economics persuades many economists and econometricians. Beyond this audience, it might seem impressive enough to overawe some, but may equally be dismissed by others.

The reason for the resistance may be found by noting the focus of logic on proof, and rhetoric on persuasion. McCloskey's *The rhetoric of economics* is now in its second edition (McCloskey 1998). It may have proved its point (the arguments are logical), but it has not persuaded many economists (the rhetoric is weak).

In economic theory, little attention is generally paid to processes and persuasion. This is perhaps inevitable, given the focus on static analysis and assumptions of exogenous preferences and rationality. However, persuasion may be important in terms of both the understanding of economic phenomena and the development of economics as a discipline.

There is other literature that incorporates concepts such as traction, agenda setting and framing. This literature shows clearly that it is not enough simply to present a correct argument. The diverse literature is more recent than that on rhetoric and considers persuasion in a broad sense, as compared to the traditional perspective of winning an argument or winning over an audience. The term 'rhetoric' is generally not expressly used, but I have collectively described the approaches as 'macro-rhetoric' (Birks 2014a). One reference that addresses these issues in a political context is Cobb and Ross (1997). Their title, *Cultural strategies*

---

[4] Note that 'proof' in law is not proof. Rather, it is persuasion of a judge or jury to interpret the evidence in a desired way.

of agenda denial: Avoidance, attack, and redefinition, suggests that there are reasons why people with a heavy investment in established positions may be unwilling to change. This is illustrated by the discussion on accepting or rejecting a theory in Chap. 2. The point has been frequently made and illustrated elsewhere. To quote Simon, 'Legitimacy may sometimes be achieved (and even attention secured) by the usual credentials of science…[b]ut many an impeccable report is ignored, and many a report without proper credentials gains a high place on the agenda' (Simon 1971, p. 50). Note also:

> Science can destroy religion by ignoring it as well as by disproving its tenets. No one ever demonstrated, so far as I am aware, the nonexistence of Zeus or Thor, but they have few followers now. (Clarke 1953, p. 21)

And, '[M]ost papers are never read at all. No matter what a paper did to the former literature, if no one else does anything else with it, then it is as if it had never existed at all'. (Latour 1987, p. 40)

Reasoned assessment may prove to be complex also, as indicated by Pope John Paul II:

> [T]here are in the life of a human being many more truths which are simply believed than truths which are acquired by way of personal verification…This means that the human being—the one who seeks the truth—is also *the one who lives by belief.* (Pope John Paul II 1998, para.31)

Political motivation on gender issues is suggested by Margaret Mayman when she said:

> Stereotypical notions of femininity have tended to obscure women's violence or alternatively, it has been actively denied by feminists, both first and second-wave, because it complicates the interpretation of women's 'innocence' and non-culpability in intimate violence. (Mayman 2003)

Durie on ethnicity also cautioned that it is, 'important that the researcher should not to be captured by current ideologies that manicure a perception of the past to suit a current purpose' (Durie 1999). This may also help to explain why the figures from one New Zealand study on the economic costs of family violence (Snively 1994) continue to be used despite the study having serious flaws (Birks 2000), whereas a PhD thesis identifying gender biases in sentencing (Jeffries 2001) has had little impact.

In relation to challenges to statistical significance, economists may still be involved in Cobb and Ross's 'avoidance'. They write of 'identification groups', people who raise an issue in the first place, and 'attention groups' who then promote the issues more widely (Cobb and Ross 1997, p. 7). Without the latter, the issue will not get off the ground. For statistical significance, sizeable attention groups may not exist. Cobb and Ross's more detailed four-level formulation (identification groups, the attentive public and attention groups, and the mass public) has parallels with an earlier description by Bryce of:

> …three classes of person who have to do with the making of public opinion…the men who seriously occupy themselves with public affairs…those who, though comparatively passive,

> take an interest in politics...[and] all that large residue of the citizens which is indifferent to public affairs, reading little and thinking less about them. (Bryce 1929, pp. 176–177)

Other writers have also identified the need for a small pressure group to gain wider support if it is to have influence. Hence, '...this kind of group is wholly dependent on the socialization of conflict...this is a trigger organisation which may start a chain reaction...' (Schattschneider 1960, pp. 47–48). Those wondering about the dominance of particular approaches in economics may find some possible explanations in perspectives such as these. Dominant groups have wider support, such as through the adoption of key textbooks and the status of particular journals. This also gives some clues as to how change might occur.

1.2.2 Framing

Central to an understanding of the significance of Fig. 1.1 and the associated potential errors is the concept of *framing*. This is generally not expressly considered by economists, but it is heavily used elsewhere (Scheufele and Tewksbury 2007; Severin and Tankard 1997; Tversky and Kahneman 1981; Weaver 2007). It has been described as a process of '*selection, emphasis, exclusion, and elaboration*' (Severin and Tankard 1997, p. 320). Choices are made (sometimes by default through the adoption of an approach) as to what will be included and excluded, and the stories which will be told about the included aspects.

Minsky (2011) is noted for his work on financial markets and economic crises. He is well aware of the problems that framing can cause, although he does not use the term. He draws on an address by Tobin (1966), to describe its significance in an economics context, writing:

> James Tobin, who was a member of the Council of Economic Advisers during President Kennedy's first 2 years in office and who received the Nobel Prize in 1982, noted that 'The terms in which a problem is stated and in which the relevant information is organized can have a great influence on the solution.' But the way 'a problem' is stated and the identification of 'relevant information' reflect the economic theory of the policy adviser. That is, the game of policymaking is rigged; the theory used determines the questions that are asked and the options that are presented. (Minsky 2008, p. 110)

The representation is one of people looking at something. Minsky states this explicitly:

> In all disciplines theory plays a double role: it is **both a lens and a blinder**. As a lens, it focuses the mind upon specified problems, enabling conditional statements be made about causal relations for a well-defined but limited set of phenomena. But as a blinder, theory narrows the field of vision. (Minsky 2008, p. 109, emphasis added)

How we look at something shapes what we see. Kuhn (1970) popularised the term '*paradigm*', which also suggests a perspective taken and has been influential in shaping current understanding of the nature of scientific enquiry (Dow 2012). However, it could be argued that these representations of the processes followed are themselves misleading. In particular, an interpretation in terms of a chosen paradigm and occasional paradigm shifts could be seen to suggest that there should be only one accepted approach at a time.

Any description, including Kuhn's (and mine) involves framing. Economic models are not representations of the real world. They are simplistic structures which could be more accurately described as *analogies* for aspects of the real world.[5] Hence, 'a 'theory' is not a collection of assertions about the behavior of the actual economy but rather an explicit set of instructions for building a parallel or analogue system' (Lucas 1980, p. 697). Theories are alternative representations which, it is hoped, under some circumstances provide information which can be a useful aid for understanding real-world events. Their applicability in any specific situation is open to question, and they will not be complete depictions of the phenomena of interest. The term 'analogy' suggests an incomplete representation and the possibility of several alternatives, and so may convey a more open picture than is given by the term 'paradigm'.

Further interpretation of the context in which economics research is undertaken can be drawn from literature on groups and group cultures. This is indicated by Kuhn with his reference to 'normal science', and by Galbraith (1999) when he talks of 'conventional wisdom'. This aspect is covered in more detail in Chap. 2.

This leads me to the key point to be taken from this book, namely that economics should be broadly defined, encompassing alternative theoretical perspectives, and seen as providing a wide range of tools. This provides a *tool kit* comprising a collection of concepts, structures, theoretical and empirical findings which are not enough on their own, but which, if properly used and applied with care, may give some insights which can help in understanding the real world and the ways in which real-world processes and outcomes can be affected. Of course, this is itself an analogy,[6] but, to repeat Minsky above, the way an issue is viewed, 'determines the questions asked and the options raised'. More specifically, with this framing and given a real-world issue to be investigated or a problem to be solved, it can be asked which selection, from all the tools available, may be most suited to the purpose.

It could also be asked how the chosen tools should they be applied. This is important. Even from the way economics is often taught, it is commonly suggested that a straight application of some chosen theory or estimation of a model is all that is required for the conduct of research. This may have become such a strong convention that some economists fail to see beyond it. It may be all that is required for publication in peer-reviewed journals, but that does not make it sufficient for guiding real-world decisions.

---

[5] No representation, whether a mathematical model, an econometric equation or set of equations, a graph, or a verbal description of a structure, is presenting a picture of the real world. They are all alternative structures. Whenever these are used to make claims about the real world, they are therefore being used as analogies.

[6] A more common perspective is to require economics research to conform to fixed conventions and rules.

Tools have limitations, and so there are constraints on what can be done. Not many decades ago it was thought, wrongly, that large econometric models would be able to provide accurate forecasts. Policy instruments were thought sensitive enough for 'fine tuning' the economy to be seen as a realistic aim. Over-ambitious, inflated claims are not unusual, especially in political environments.

Even within the boundaries of what can be achieved, tools do not do the whole job. A combination of tools over a number of processes may be required, and even that is not the whole story. As Keynes has written, 'where we are not blindly manipulating but know all the time what we are doing and what the words mean, we can keep 'at the back of our heads' the necessary *reserves and qualifications and the adjustments* which we shall have to make later on' (Keynes 2007, p. 297). With the application of any economic analysis, there are reservations and qualifications to be made and further adjustments needed.

My message is a positive one, in that there are a lot of tools available. They should be applied with thought and with care, recognising their strengths and weaknesses, and incorporating additional deliberation. This will provide the means to undertake flexible and powerful analyses which can increase understanding and have real-world relevance.

References

Aristotle (1954) Rhetoric ([1st Modern Library] ed.). Modern Library, New York

Birks S (2000) Comments on the economic cost of family violence. In: Birks S, Buurman G (eds) Research for policy: informing or misleading. Centre for Public Policy Evaluation, Massey University, Palmerston North, pp 17–25

Birks S (2014a). Rethinking economics: downs with traction. World Econ Rev 3:37–52. http://wer.worldeconomicsassociation.org/files/WEA-WER-3-Birks.pdf

Bryce J (1929) Modern democracies, vol 1. Macmillan, London

Chang H-J (2014) Economics: the user's guide. Pelican, London

Clarke AC (1953) Childhood's end. Harcourt, Brace and World, New York

Cobb RW, Ross MH (eds) (1997) Cultural strategies of agenda denial: avoidance, attack, and redefinition. University Press of Kansas, Lawrence

Dow SC (2012) Foundations for new economic thinking: a collection of essays. Palgrave Macmillan, Houndmills

Dunn WN (2004) Public policy analysis: an introduction, 3rd edn. Pearson Prentice Hall, Upper Saddle River

Durie ET (1999) Ethics and values. Indigenous peoples and the law, (November). http://www.kennett.co.nz/law/indigenous/1999/39.html

Galbraith JK (1999) The affluent society, New edn. Penguin, London

Gillies D (2006) Why research assessment exercises are a bad thing. Post-autistic Econ Rev 37:2–9. http://www.paecon.net/PAEReview/issue37/Gillies37.htm

Jeffries S (2001) Gender judgments: an investigation of gender differentiation in sentencing and remand in New Zealand. University of Canterbury, Christchurch

Kay J (2011) The map is not the territory: an essay on the state of economics. http://ineteconomics.org/sites/inet.civicactions.net/files/kay-john-state-of-economics-v11.pdf

Keynes JM (2007) The general theory of employment, interest, and money, New edn. Palgrave Macmillan, Basingstoke

Klamer A (2007) Speaking of economics: how to get in the conversation. Routledge, New York

Kuhn TS (1970) The structure of scientific revolutions, 2nd edn. University of Chicago Press, Chicago

Latour B (1987) Science in action: how to follow scientists and engineers through society. Harvard University Press, Cambridge

Lawson T (1997) Economics and reality. Routledge, London

Lawson T (2003) Reorienting economics. Routledge, London

Lucas RE Jr (1980) Methods and problems in business cycle theory. J Money Credit Banking 12 (4):696–715. doi:10.2307/1992030

Mayman M (2003) Raised voices: ending intimate violence: lecture two—heroes of their own lives: women and children empowered (2 December). http://satrs.standrews.org.nz/mmiv2of2.doc

McCloskey DN (1998) The rhetoric of economics (2nd ed.). University of Wisconsin Press, Madison

Minsky HP (2008) Stabilizing an unstable economy, New edn. McGraw-Hill, New York

Minsky HP (2011) The financial instability hypothesis. In: Stilwell FJB, Argyrous G (eds) Readings in political economy: economics as a social science, 3rd edn. Tilda University Press, Prahan, pp 183–186

Pope John Paul II (1998) Encyclical letter fides et ratio of the Supreme Pontiff John Paul II to the Bishops of the Catholic Church on the relationship between faith and reason (September 14). http://www.vatican.va/holy_father/john_paul_ii/encyclicals/documents/hf_jp-ii_enc_15101998_fides-et-ratio_en.html

Schattschneider EE (1960) The semisovereign people; a realist's view of democracy in America. Holt, Rinehart and Winston, New York

Scheufele DA, Tewksbury D (2007) Framing, agenda setting, and priming: the evolution of three media effects models. J Commun 57(1):9–20

Schopenhauer A (1851) The art of controversy. Retrieved from http://etext.library.adelaide.edu.au/s/schopenhauer/arthur/controversy/

Severin WJ, Tankard JW (1997) Communication theories: origins, methods, and uses in the mass media, 4th edn. Longman, New York

Simon HA (1971) Designing organisations for an information-rich world. In: Greenberger M (ed) Computers, communications, and the public interest. The Johns Hopkins Press, Baltimore, pp 38–52

Smith A (1963) Lectures on rhetoric and belles lettres: delivered in the University of Glasgow by Adam Smith, reported by a student in 1762–63. Nelson, London

Snively SL (1994) The New Zealand economic cost of family violence. Family Violence Unit, Dept. of Social Welfare, Wellington

Tobin J (1966) The intellectual revolution in U.S. policy making [Noel Boxton Lectures]. University of Essex, Essex

Tversky A, Kahneman D (1981) The framing of decisions and the psychology of choice. Science 211(4481):453–458

Weaver DH (2007) Thoughts on agenda setting, framing, and priming. J Commun 57(1):142–147

Ziliak ST, McCloskey DN (2008) The cult of statistical significance: how the standard error costs us jobs, justice, and lives. University of Michigan Press, Ann Arbor

Chapter 2
Logical Gaps: Path A—Theory to the Real World

Abstract Many claims are widely accepted because they have been demonstrated to be valid according to some theory. However, while theories are, hopefully, internally consistent, they can be considered no more than analogies for the real world. This chapter explores this dimension, including discussion of rhetoric used in support of preferred theories. Perfect competition and Tversky and Kahneman's 'systematic reversals of preference' are used to illustrate these points, including the limitation of consistency as justification for acceptance of a theory. The importance of groups to create and establish dominant conventions is also covered.

Keywords Theory · Analogy · Framing · Counterfactual · Groups · Rhetoric

Controversially, in his classic essay, 'The methodology of positive economics', Friedman (1953) talks of the realism of assumptions not being important. It is only necessary that the resulting models 'predict well'. In other words, given behavioural assumptions of rational, utility maximising individuals, for example, it is enough that they behave 'as if' they are rational and utility maximising. This influential essay has been used to support a possibly damaging development, the use of theories based on unrealistic assumptions. In his Preface to *The general theory of employment, interest, and money* Keynes wrote:

> For if orthodox economics is at fault, the error is to be found not in the superstructure, which has been erected with great care for logical consistency, but in a lack of clearness and of generality in the premisses. (Keynes 2007, p. xv)

Path A suggests that theory does not describe the real world. Theory presents a simplified structure that, hopefully, is a suitable analogy for certain aspects of the real world. Extra thought is required for the application of theory. This point was illustrated in October 2008, when there was a coordinated international response to what had been recognised as a global financial crisis. On 23 October in the US, the former chairman of the Federal Reserve, Alan Greenspan., appeared before the House Oversight and Government Affairs Committee, where he read a statement (Greenspan 2008) and answered questions. In the statement he described, his understanding of the reasons for the 'once-in-a-century credit tsunami' arising from

S. Birks, *Rethinking Economics*, SpringerBriefs in Economics,
DOI 10.1007/978-981-287-176-3_2

the subprime mortgage crisis. Here is an extract from an exchange between him and the chairman of the committee, Rep. Henry Waxman:

WAXMAN	You found a flaw in the reality
GREENSPAN	Flaw in the model that I perceived as the critical functioning structure that defines how the world works
WAXMAN	In other words, you found that your view of the world, your ideology was not right
GREENSPAN	Precisely

(F. James 2008)

Greenspan was treating his chosen theoretical perspective as if it were representative of the real world. In general, people's perceptions of their environment can be shaped by many things, including their education, the views of their discipline, beliefs within a discipline, commonly promoted views in the news media, and concepts of acceptable reasoning. Issues are not analysed simply on the evidence presented for that particular issue. The analysis is shaped by numerous other influences that individuals bring with them to interpret that evidence, with theories being an important component.

While theory is important in shaping understanding, its influence can be misplaced. This suggests a need to investigate the nature and function of theory as a means of understanding real world events.

2.1 What Is Theory?

Theory, and in particular economic theory, can be seen as a tool for analysing issues and presenting criteria for evaluation of alternatives. It has limitations, so the nature of theory should be recognised. Any theory involves simplification, giving a partial view based on a particular perspective. It is at best an approximation of reality. Alternative theories highlight different aspects and give differing results. This difference in emphasis can be most apparent when comparing theories across disciplines, but differences are more commonly identified and debated between competing schools of the same discipline. A possible outcome of these differences is described in the poem about the blind men and the elephant, where each man felt a different part of the elephant, drawing their own conclusions as to the appearance of the animal (like a wall, like a tree…) (Saxe 1878). The image is significant, especially in the way that each person in the poem attempted to describe the elephant in terms of some other object that they knew, that they could use as an analogy. Any specific issue can be considered by several disciplines, schools within disciplines, and professions. Each one applies its own existing body of knowledge, perspectives, and tools of analysis. It also focuses on the use of its own set of potential instruments or policy variables. They are looking at the same thing, but in different ways and with differing conclusions.

Theories are commonly presented in terms of variables and the relationships between them, so that, at their core, there is a model. This would fit a conventional view of theory in economics. A model is a simplified representation that is intended to highlight the main elements of a phenomenon. Except for possible differences in the level of formalisation, it is not unlike the approach that a person might take on any issue, as in adopting a stylized, simplified or heuristic representation of the real world.

From one perspective, the use of theoretical findings might be considered as merely a 'mode of argumentation', such as Dunn's Mode No. 5, reasoning from cause, 'For example, a claim may be made based on general propositions, or laws of economics that state invariant relations between cause and effect' (Dunn 2004, p. 395). The following discussions of models illustrate this alternative, considering them as forms of **analogy**, **metaphor** and **attribute agenda setting** or **framing**.

Klamer, in an economics context, describes a model as, 'an explicitly, and in economics often formally, articulated **analogy**. A model is typically characterised by "as if" reasoning' (Klamer 2007, p. 123). It was not by accident that the blind men each interpreted their impression of the elephant by means of analogy. Lakoff and Johnson, from a linguistic perspective, focus on the use of metaphor to describe the way that people develop an understanding, where, 'The essence of **metaphor** is understanding and experiencing one kind of thing in terms of another' (Lakoff and Johnson 2003, p. 5). With economic models, economic phenomena are commonly expressed in terms of mathematical/mechanical systems. Lakoff and Johnson speak more generally:

> In all aspects of life…we define our reality in terms of metaphors and then proceed to act on the basis of the metaphors. We draw inferences, set goals, make commitments, and execute plans, all on the basis of how we in part structure our experience, consciously and unconsciously, by means of metaphor. (Lakoff and Johnson 2003, p. 158)

They distinguish between direct and indirect experience, where indirect experience involves some additional processing or interpretation of information in order to derive meaning. Hence feelings of pain, or hot and cold, are direct, but interpretation of a remark as a complement or an insult requires some assessment of context and point of comparison. Consequently for indirect experiences people are, 'understanding *one kind* of entity or experience in terms of *another kind*—that is, understanding via metaphor.' (Lakoff and Johnson 2003, p. 178) Broader policy issues can be entirely indirect, lacking any direct personal experience at all, so metaphors or analogies are important. A metaphor highlights certain aspects, 'and what is not highlighted is downplayed or hidden' (Lakoff and Johnson 2003, p. 179). So models and theories could be considered as metaphors which shape perceptions and understanding, with many aspects being hidden.

Communication literature refers to **frames**. Hence Severin and Tankard, discussing the news media, write (emphasis added), A frame can be defined as 'a central organising idea for news content that supplies a context and suggests what the issue is through the use of **selection**, **emphasis**, **exclusion**, and **elaboration**'

(Severin and Tankard 1997, p. 320).[1] As with analogy and metaphor, framing can be widely observed. In fact, theories and models could be considered as frames, involving these four components of selection, etc. Similar points are made in a political context by Cobb and Ross (1997). They describe agenda setting and denial, whereby groups attempt to set the agenda to attend to their issues and ignore those of other groups. Weaver (2007) takes this approach with an additional distinction between the selection of issues (what) and the choice of perspective on the issues (how), the latter being likened to framing. Fairclough (1995) on discourse analysis identifies 'ideological-discursive formations' (IDFs) with which groups may use a choice of language to favour their perspective, given that the terms used, and their associated connotations, shape perceptions. Mainstream economists have their own IDF, including the concept of 'market failure', which is the product of framing in terms of it being a failure to achieve the claimed optimality of a society experiencing perfect competition everywhere.

To summarise, various bodies of literature have their own terms for very similar phenomena. They all suggest that understanding is influenced by the perspectives taken, and theories and models perform this function also. As they affect perceptions, they may result in distorted understanding. Rhetoric may have an undue influence, as discussed by Dunn. It is inevitable that theories and models will be used to aid understanding, but they are not accurate representations of the real world. They are alternative structures which, it is hoped, may bear some resemblance to, and provide some insight into real world phenomena. However, they are partial, they may distort, and they may mislead. It is important that the nature of theories and, in particular, their limitations be understood. Otherwise, the theories might be considered, wrongly, as definitive descriptions of real world situations. In short, theories should be treated as analogies for, not representations of, the real world.

2.2 Limits of Theory

As mentioned above, mainstream microeconomic theory focuses heavily on the concept of 'market failure'. It plays an important role in economic arguments for policy selection. As the underlying assumptions and theory are questioned by heterodox economists (Earl 1995; Hodgson 2001; Keen 2001; Komlos 2014; Lawson 2003; Mearman 2007; Stretton 1999; Tomer 2001) and non-economists

---

[1] Note that the term 'frame' has been used in a different context to mean a 'conceptual frame' (Bateson 1972; Goffman 1974). Bateson (1972, p. 182) describes fighting that is not intended to injure, suggesting that this could be seen as 'play' or as 'ritual'. The nature of the relationship between a doctor and a patient might be perceived differently when framed as one between a health care provider and a consumer of health care. Depending on their conceptual framing of the situation, the parties each have perceptions of their respective roles and hence expected behaviours. Particular problems can arise when perceptions do not match.

(Bosso 1994; Considine 2005; Dunn 2004), the issue merits some attention.[2] More generally, given that there may be several possible explanations of observed phenomena, care should be taken about any conclusions that rely on evidence being 'consistent with' theory. There may be numerous alternative explanations of the observed phenomena that can be presented. These two points, perfect competition and consistency, are considered here.

2.2.1 Perfect Competition and Counterfactuals

Market failure is defined in comparison to the ideal of perfect competition. An alternative is needed for comparison, and value judgments must be applied to justify one situation being considered superior to another. This raises two questions:

(i) Is perfect competition the right 'ideal'?
(ii) If it is, then given that the counterfactual is an important aspect of any policy analysis, should economic analyses compare a real situation with an unattainable ideal such as perfect competition?

Theory is, in essence, an intellectual exercise, whereby structures are presented and implications drawn. There is no a *priori* reason to assume that they in any way accurately reflect, or even closely approximate, the real world.[3] Sen summarised the situation in his paper on 'Rational Fools' (Sen 1977). In it he described Edgeworth's analysis on the possibility of egoistic behaviour achieving general good as an abstract query, not intended to reflect reality. Economists have taken something that was intended as an intellectual exercise, paradoxically extending it to become a combined answer to questions of 'how people actually behave' and 'how people should behave'.[4]

Its origins aside, why should there be a reluctance to take the perfect competition model as the basis for an ideal structure in society? There are several reasons:

---

[2] Note also that there are older, more specific critiques such as criticism of the 'postulational method', theory built on postulates (Koopmans 1957; Kurien 1970), In addition, a reading of the classics, not least Smith (2007), indicates a highly nuanced assessment, much of which has been lost in current textbook expositions.

[3] At a most basic level, considering the distinction between ontology and epistemology, any description relies on the classifications afforded by the mode of expression, as with the use of language. There is not a one-to-one correspondence between words in different languages. Even if there were, the link from language to the phenomena that the words describe is not precise, if only because of the aggregation and discrete distinctions implicit in language. Consequently, descriptions cannot precisely reflect the real world.

[4] This is a serious paradox. Is no education required to improve people's economic decision making? If so, why is it accepted that education is required to increase understanding in other areas of activity? In any event, can economic decisions be considered in isolation?

1. It is static analysis. It does not consider a starting point. While there are initial endowments, these have yet to be allocated. Consequently, it overlooks issues of adjustment paths and the cost and time of adjustment. It also provides an optimum, on the given criteria, for that scenario. This is not the same as an optimum path through time. Such an optimum path may not equate to a series of static optima. For example disequilibria are associated with plans not being realised, and therefore some people having an incentive to change. Consider change through innovation, for example and Schumpeter's competition through 'creative destruction':

   > A system—any system, economic or other—that at every given point of time fully utilises its possibilities to the best advantage may yet in the long run be inferior to a system that does so at no given point of time, because the latter's failure to do so may be a condition for the level or speed of long-run performance. (Schumpeter 1976, p. 83)

   Conversely, the idea of change under perfect competition is simply in terms of adjustment to a static optimum. It is actually very brutal. If demand falls, in the long-run firms leave the market, with any costs of exit being ignored. If demand rises, it is assumed that there are always entrepreneurs able and willing to enter the market. In other words, there is free and costless entry and exit, which is simply not the case in reality. The effects of change should be considered, and in some circumstances, the result of disequilibria may be superior to that from a static equilibrium position.
2. Comparisons are based on comparative static analysis, comparing two static situations. This does not include consideration of whether it is actually possible to move from one position to the other, or that there is a starting situation from which change is required.
3. It has a very narrow perspective on people's objectives, with individual utility maximisers where utility comes solely from the consumption of goods and services and is funded through the supply of factors of production.
4. The focus is solely on the end result rather than any consideration of the ways in which the end result is achieved. This is an example of consequentialism, where 'the end justifies the means'. However, in reality there may be justified concerns about the nature of the operations through which an outcome arises. Much of our time is spent in the attainment of goals rather than the enjoyment of the goals once they are reached.
5. It is assumed that all interactions will be by law-abiding individuals accepting property rights with no political influences and no prejudices and no strategic behaviour. It excludes the possibility of behaviour as might be found, for example when some countries impose sanctions on another for doing something that they disagree with. There are issues with the use of law to enforce agreements, and problems with the choice of laws and jurisdictions that apply in international contexts. There is the cost of administering and enforcing compliance with the structures that are set, and difficulties in determining contracts. All these issues are assumed away, with compliant behaviour costlessly achieved.

6. It assumes that society can be viewed as a system of markets, ignoring any other dimensions of decision-making and resource allocation, such as the public, political or social. For an alternative view, consider:

> Markets and governments are both facts of economic life, and they interact in complex ways. We cannot find feasible improvements by wishing away one of the components. (Dixit 1996, p. xv)

For some case studies on the sometimes significant but unrecognised role of the state in private sector activity, see Mazzucato (2013).

Now let us consider the issue of counterfactuals. Aristotle (350 B.C E.: Part 1) discussed the limitations of unattainable optima, and Demsetz. makes a similar point, using the term 'nirvana approach'.[5] In epidemiology, four alternatives have been suggested as counterfactuals in relation to risk of disease. These are *theoretical minimum risk*, *plausible minimum risk*, *feasible minimum risk* and *cost-effective minimum risk* (Murray and Lopez 1999). These represent, in turn, the lowest risk imaginable, even if highly unrealistic; the lowest risk that might be considered possible, even if not currently realistic; the lowest risk that has been achieved somewhere, and thus is known to be attainable; and the lowest risk that could be achieved using all cost-effective means available. The economic 'ideal' as a counterfactual would roughly parallel the theoretical minimum risk, containing no distortions, while the others reflect the best that one might ever expect to achieve, or the best that has been observed elsewhere, or the best that could be currently achieved using approaches that are known to be cost-effective. When the choice of counterfactual is framed in this way, perfect competition stands out as an extreme option.

Additional dimensions could be considered in a policy setting when selecting counterfactuals. For example the timing of the alternatives, political acceptability, distribution of costs and benefits and certainty of outcome may be relevant. Nor should the Theory of Second Best (Lipsey and Lancaster 1956) be overlooked. This theory effectively means that the elimination of a distortion (such as a market failure) does not necessarily result in an improvement. Keen (2001) illustrates this point well in his example of an economy with a monopolist and a trade union. It may not be desirable to eliminate one only, leaving the other in place. In other words, perhaps some other goal should be chosen, as suggested by the alternative counterfactuals, although there may be significant information requirements that would have to be met to achieve second best outcomes.

To summarise, there is a possibility that economics is using as an optimum something that would not be meaningful, desirable, or widely accepted. Even if the chosen optimum is suitable as an ideal, that may not be a useful criterion for

---

[5] 'The view that now pervades much public policy economics implicitly presents the relevant choice as between an ideal norm and an existing "imperfect" institutional arrangement. This nirvana approach differs considerably from a comparative institution approach in which the relevant choice is between alternative real institutional arrangements' (Demsetz 1969, p. 1).

judging failures and interventions. Given the rhetoric of economics, it is necessary to explain these potential weaknesses. Recognition of them then opens up the possibility of other criteria and consideration of other aspects to be considered. Also, to avoid Type A errors, it is necessary to investigate issues beyond those assumed within particular theoretical models.

2.2.2 Accepting or Rejecting a Theory

Theories serve as tools that may aid in attempts to understand the real world environment and to make decisions. As with any tools, care must be taken in their use. There are alternative views on how those who favour a theory can or should react to criticisms of that theory. Three arguments that are sometimes used in response to such criticisms are described below. They all have flaws and can lead to problems. A fourth option is then discussed. The four options are:

(1) Accept current theory as a matter of faith;
(2) Do not look outside current theory as long as it can give SOME explanation of an observed phenomenon;
(3) Do not reject a theory, even if flawed, unless the challenger can present a superior alternative;
(4) Take a more pragmatic approach.

We can consider these four views in turn.

(1) Accept current theory as a matter of faith

Several writers have voiced concern at a perceived debasement of academic standards. Mishan talked of 'the stringent requirements of scholarship' being set aside where, 'the doctrines of… ideologically inspired "studies" are not regarded by their proponents as provisional and refutable hypotheses' (Mishan 1993, p. 202). This suggests the possibility of a higher level of academic discourse. Mishan was referring to studies based on gender and ethnicity. However, similar criticisms could also be made against other academics, even without clear political motivation, or rather, through acknowledging the politics of academia. Economics may also fit this description. Hence, 'Factual evidence to the contrary, and arguments, however convincing, are unlikely to destroy faith in the "validity" of a theory widely accepted for a long time' (Kurien 1970, p. 34).

A possible explanation lies in the effect of the framing of economic theory. The suggestion in this context would be that, while economic theory may be based on 'provisional and refutable hypotheses', the basis may seldom be questioned, and it may even be considered that the issues have been fully debated and resolved, or, at least, so well entrenched as to be accepted as a starting point for any analysis. This would match the concepts of a 'dominant IDF' (Fairclough 1995), 'normal science' (Kuhn 1970) , and 'conventional wisdom' (Galbraith 1999) and has been described specifically for economics (Robinson 1970; Rosen 1972).

It could be said of the dominant mainstream theory that economic theory provides frames that have come to be widely accepted among economists, and these shape perceptions of economic phenomena. Being accepted, they both enlighten and restrict the aspects that are observed. Taking a step back, one could consider whether economic theory has tended to set the agenda itself. In other words, dominant perspectives in economics have determined not only the approaches to issues, but also the selection of issues and questions to be considered (and those to be overlooked) by economists.

(2) Do not look outside current theory as long as it can give SOME explanation of an observed phenomenon

Normal science has been described as, 'a strenuous and devoted attempt to force nature into the conceptual boxes supplied by a professional education' (Kuhn 1970, p. 5). Similarly, 'conservative conventionalists attempt to preserve existent theories by building onto them ever more elaborate (critics would label them ad hoc) peripheral systems' (Caldwell 1980, p. 367). Even if successful, it should not be considered as an end to discussion. Not only is the presence of alternative consistent hypotheses possible, but, according to Milton Friedman, it is inevitable:

> Observed facts are necessarily finite in number; possible hypotheses, infinite. If there is one hypothesis that is consistent with the available evidence, there are always an infinite number that are. (Friedman 1953, p. 9)

This criterion for acceptability of an established theory, simply being consistent with the evidence, sets the bar at such a low level that many theories would be virtually impossible to reject. This could lead to an inflated view of the level of understanding, and may be one reason why economists are sometimes thought of as arrogant.

(3) Do not reject a theory, even if flawed, unless the challenger can present a superior alternative

Writing on econometrics in *The Economic Journal*, Phillips quotes Hoover, who makes a claim about scientists: 'even accumulated falsifications or anomalies do not cause scientists to abandon an approach unless there is the prospect of a better approach on offer' (Phillips 2003, p. C27). The point is made for economics, '... you can't beat something with nothing, and so it is not enough to show that some given rational choice model does not fit the data, it is necessary to show that some other perspective leads to a model with better fit and predictive power' (Grofman 1993, p. 240). This approach would support the use of something that is known to be misleading in preference to admitting ignorance. Criticisms of a theory or the presentation of contrary evidence have been dismissed on the basis that a superior alternative has not been presented. However, while this is effective rhetoric, it is not a valid reason for ignoring flaws in a theory. Socrates, 2,400 years ago, made the point that it is important to recognise the limits of one's understanding (Plato, Approx 380 B.C.E.). Disciplinary boundaries, where adhered to and where this rhetoric is used to dismiss criticism, can serve to perpetuate misconceptions and to limit fruitful imagination.

(4) Take a more pragmatic approach

The three views above could be considered as being logically flawed. Alternatively, they could be described as rhetorical arguments that are persuasive for their target audiences. They are widely used by people who want to maintain a particular position. However, there is another option available. The information for the public on the 2008 award of the Nobel Prize to Krugman includes the statement, 'The truth, as in so many other instances, is that reality encompasses features of both theories' (The Royal Swedish Academy of Sciences 2008, p. 2). Similarly, Tullock writes, 'I have given you a number of theories on how regulatory agencies act and I regret to say that instead of telling you now which one of them is true, I think all of them are partly true' (Tullock et al. 1983, p. 10). There is a danger that a focus on simple explanations, automatically assuming they are valid, not looking beyond a narrow, accepted perspective, or rejecting valid criticisms unless alternative superior solutions are presented, results in an inflated sense of the extent to which issues are understood.

A pragmatic approach would result in a qualified use of theory-based understanding. Alternative evidence can result in two key qualifications that should be recognised:

(a) Valid criticisms should be recognised as limitations of current understanding (and hence on ability to intervene to bring about desired changes);
(b) All theories should be recognised as being partial, and they are analogies for, rather than representations of, the real world. They result in the framing of issues, so it is prudent to use a mix of theories and to acknowledge the aspects that are assumed away in a particular theoretical approach. There are additional reserves, qualifications, and adjustments to be considered in any application of theory (note Keynes 2007, p. 297).

These points can be expressed in another way. Rather than considering that there are 'theories' that may 'explain' the evidence of the real world, it should be recognised that there are 'analogies' that may be 'consistent with' the evidence of the real world (and may then in addition possess some explanatory power). To take the latter to be the former is to overstate the level and value of perceived understanding.

2.2.3 Evidence Consistent with Theory

Tversky and Kahneman are well known for a celebrated finding in behavioural economics which is considered to show that a basic assumption in economics does not hold. They suggest that people violate rational choice requirements of consistency and coherence due to 'psychological principles that govern the perception of decision problems and the evaluation of options', such that, 'We have obtained systematic reversals of preference by variations in the framing of acts, contingencies, or outcomes' (Tversky and Kahneman 1981, p. 453). The use of the term 'framing' is worth noting. In their summary, they suggest that, 'The dependence of preferences on the formulation of decision problems is a significant concern for the theory of rational choice' (Tversky and Kahneman 1981, p. 453).

Their finding is illustrated by their now classic example of the outbreak of an unusual Asian disease which is expected to kill 600 people. Two scenarios are given. First, the options are:

- Program A, 200 people will be saved
- Program B, there is 1/3 probability that 600 people will be saved, and 2/3 probability that no people will be saved

There is a strong preference for option A. For the second scenario, another group is given options C and D:

- Program C, 400 people will die
- Program D, there is 1/3 probability that nobody will die, and 2/3 probability that 600 people will die.

There is then a strong preference for option D.

Tversky and Kahneman suggest that the outcomes in the two problems are actually identical because the numbers living and dying in each option are the same. They then assume that the framing is distorting because it shapes perceptions differently. This assumption is key to their finding. Their interpretation of result has been widely accepted. For example, 'Tversky and Kahneman's 1981 study…is the gold standard for demonstrating the effects of framing on behavior: identical events, different metaphors, flipped decision" (Pinker 2007, p. 244)'. However, there are other possible explanations. Consider, as a basis for these alternatives, that the payoffs to the decision maker may not be specified in terms of lives saved or lost (under which the two problems are identical), but are linked to perceptions of the choices. These may differ over the two problems. To illustrate, in the first scenario, the focus is on the 200 who could be saved with certainty, in which event option B would involve risking the lives of these people. In the second scenario, by contrast, the focus is on the 400 who would face certain death under program C, but who might be saved under program D. The choice of the risky option is then one of possibly saving these 400 from otherwise certain death. Here are two alternative hypotheses, others are discussed by Altman (2008).

For one hypothesis, Tyler (2000, p. 123) has suggested that people may accept different treatment of people according to group membership.[6] In this case, two groups are defined, with one group emphasized in the first formulation and the other emphasized in the second. If the decision makers are led to identify with the first

---

[6] Others have found groups to be important for perceptions and behaviour (Weng and Yang 2014). This point is discussed further in Sect. 2.2.4.

group, the certain survivors, they may not wish to risk their lives. If they identify with the second group, the certain fatalities, they may choose the risky option in an attempt to save them.

For a second hypothesis, participants may interpret the difference in the framing of the options as reflecting society's preferences, and hence the pay-offs they would face. Pay-offs depend on other people's perceptions, and are measured in terms of these other people's responses. A choice of the risky option could then result in being seen by others (their superiors, or public opinion, say) as risking the lives of the 200, and possibly being blamed for causing their deaths. Alternatively, it could be seen as trying to save 400 from certain death, and being praised if the gamble pays off. Should they risk the lives of 200, or take a risk to try to save 400? There could be a difference in terms of praise or blame in the perceived pay-offs for the two problems.

Tversky and Kahneman write of the importance of the 'reference outcome' against which other outcomes are 'perceived as positive or negative'. 'The reference outcome is usually a state to which one has adapted; it is sometimes set by social norms and expectations…' (Tversky and Kahneman 1981, p. 456). It is only a short step from there to suggest that the decision makers will also be judged, and rewarded or penalised, according to those norms or expectations. Consideration of rationality should then focus not only on the decision-maker, but also on the society and the institutions. It should be defined not within the simplified world of the theory, but in the actual context in which the decision-makers are operating. As a general point, when it is found that evidence 'supports' a theory, it should be considered as indicating that the theory is one possible explanation of the evidence, but the analysis should not stop there. There may be numerous alternative explanations also.

2.2.4 An Additional Consideration: The Importance of Groups

Various social sciences may take different approaches to the analysis of the same phenomena. Members of a discipline (economists included) are likely to be subscribing to partial assessments that are inconsistent with those of other disciplines. Group cultures, understandings and accepted reasoning and behaviours may be significant influences on outcomes. In economics, Galbraith (1999) writes of the significance of 'conventional wisdom'. Williamson (1975) notes the importance of 'atmosphere' and 'informal group influences', and Laffont and Martimort (2001) refer to interactions between private incentives and cultural norms of behaviour. There are some well-known examples of ordinary people displaying extreme group behaviour, including the Stanford experiment where students played the roles of guards and prisoners (1999), and the Milgram experiment, where subjects were instructed to administer increasingly severe electric shocks (Milgram 1974). If such extreme behaviour can be readily engineered in these experiments, might not milder forms of attitude and behaviour formation also be common in the real world?

There is other evidence that group dynamics may be important in determining collective views and behaviour. Numerous examples were given over 150 years ago in the book, *Extraordinary popular delusions and the madness of crowds* (Mackay 1995). Even among economists, and for economics as a discipline, there may be common acceptance of the conventions despite cause for unease. Might commonly held views be as much the result of a collective group dynamic as a logical, reasoned, and regularly reviewed and revised, assessment of theory and evidence? New entrants are educated as to the established conventions, and their acceptance into the group depends on a demonstrated competence according to those conventions. Given the emphasis given to peer review, it could be asked whether it serves as quality control, or as a device for gatekeeping (Gillies 2006). This would be consistent with 'street-level epistemology' (Hardin 2002), whereby people accept the information conveyed by those around them.

Groups can be found in many places, including academic disciplines, professions, institutions, social organisations, and political parties. The previous sections of this chapter suggest that they may each have their own culture and beliefs, including unquestioned assumptions, perspectives on issues, and inertia limiting change. This affects understanding and communication across groups. It can be important both for economists as a group (or a collection of groups), and as a phenomenon which affects the operation of the economy and the political environment in which policy is made and implemented. A theoretical framework based on individuals with exogenous preferences cannot incorporate these influences.

2.3 Conclusions

The direct application of theory to real world issues requires more than just the use of logic within a theoretical structure. There are additional questions to be addressed, disregard of which results in a rhetorical dimension to the resulting advice. Central to the application of theory to the real world is the recognition that theoretical representations serve only as analogies of the real world. These are simplified and incomplete, and different approaches or perspectives may see the 'elephant' quite differently. The nature of 'theory as analogy' should be acknowledged.

This raises several concerns. One specific to mainstream economics is the use of a theoretical 'ideal' as a basis for real world policy recommendations. Such an ideal is defined within the bounds of the theory. It may not result in realistic decision-making if the theoretical relationships do not match the real world, if the theory is based on a poor measure of society's objectives, or if the theoretically derived optimum is an unattainable position. Another concern is the recognition that theories may be merely 'consistent with' the evidence. A theory that appears to explain some evidence may simply give one of numerous possible explanations, and so should not be thought sufficient to definitively resolve an issue.

There are several positions that may be observed in response to evidence that appears to conflict with a theory. Three that are described here are that a theory could be accepted as a matter of faith, it could be accepted as sufficient as long as it can be adapted to give some explanation of the evidence, or it should be retained unless an alternative explanation is provided that is considered superior. Each of these overlooks the nature of theory as an analogy, and results in limiting the investigation and probably presenting an inflated impression of the prevailing level of understanding provided by a theory.

Recognition of the limitations of the theoretical approach in general would be helpful. Any particular theory considers a limited range of factors and interactions, overlooking much of the available evidence and the thinking and analysis that exist elsewhere. The best that can be done with a theory is to demonstrate consistency with the selected observations. There may be numerous possible alternative explanations. Relaxed or changed assumptions or consideration of alternative evidence may suggest very different conclusions. Given the diverse perspectives available, all of them partial, a combination or synthesis of theories and concepts may yield a superior understanding to that of one theory alone. At the least, it could indicate the contradictions in and limitations of the diverse attempts to understand issues. These limitations should also be recognised. An analogy for the real world does not describe the real world itself.

The environment also plays a part in determining which theories are proposed and accepted. This can be seen in terms of groups and group beliefs. Group membership, including that for an academic discipline or sub-discipline, requires acceptance of a body of knowledge or beliefs and its associated perspectives and findings. These may be slow to change, and they may differ from those of other groups focusing on similar issues. Alternatively, this could be described in terms of differing agendas and framing. Consequently, there is a rhetorical dimension to positions that are taken.

This chapter indicates that caution should be exercised in the application of commonly accepted theories. Similar issues can be found in consideration of the empirical representation of theory and in the application of empirical findings to real world issues. That is the subject of the next two chapters.

References

Altman M (2008) Behavioral economics, economic theory and public policy. Australas J Econ Edu 5(1–2): 1–55

Bateson G (1972) Steps to an ecology of mind. Chandler Pub. Co, San Francisco

Bosso CJ (1994) The contextual basis of problem definition. In: Rochefort DA, Cobb RW (eds) The politics of problem definition: shaping the policy agenda. University Press of Kansas, Lawrence

Caldwell BJ (1980) A critique of Friedman's methodological instrumentalism. South Econ J 47(2): 366–374

Cobb RW, Ross MH (eds) (1997) Cultural strategies of agenda denial: avoidance, attack, and redefinition. University Press of Kansas, Lawrence

Considine M (2005) Making public policy: institutions, actors, strategies. Polity Press, Cambridge

Demsetz H (1969) Information and efficiency: another viewpoint. J Law Econ 12(1):1–22

Dixit AK (1996) The making of economic policy: a transaction-cost politics perspective. MIT Press, Cambridge

Dunn WN (2004) Public policy analysis: an introduction, 3rd edn. Pearson Prentice Hall, Upper Saddle River

Earl PE (1995) Microeconomics for business and marketing: lectures, cases, and worked essays. E. Elgar, Aldershot

Fairclough N (1995) Critical discourse analysis: the critical study of language. Longman, London

Friedman M (1953) The methodology of positive economics. In: Friedman M (ed) Essays in positive economics. University of Chicago Press, Chicago, Ill., pp 3–43

Galbraith JK (1999) The affluent society, new ed. Penguin, London

Gillies D (2006) Why research assessment exercises are a bad thing. Post-autistic Econo Rev 37: 2–9. http://www.paecon.net/PAEReview/issue37/Gillies37.htm

Goffman E (1974) Frame analysis: an essay on the organization of experience. Harvard University Press, Cambridge

Greenspan A (2008) Testimony to the committee of government oversight and reform, Oct 23. http://oversight-archive.waxman.house.gov/documents/20081023100438.pdf. Accessed 13 June 2014

Grofman B (1993) On the gentle art of rational choice bashing. In: Grofman B (ed) Information, participation, and choice: an economic theory of democracy in perspective. University of Michigan Press, Ann Arbor

Hardin R (2002) Street-level epistemology and democratic participation. J Polit Philos 10(2): 212–229

Hodgson GM (2001) How economics forgot history: the problem of historical specificity in social science. Routledge, New York

James F (2008, 23 October). Greenspan: Money mess rocked his world. http://www.swamppolitics.com/news/politics/blog/2008/10/greenspan_money_mess_rocked_hi.html. Accessed 24 Oct 2008

Keen S (2001) Debunking economics: the naked emperor of the social sciences. Pluto Press, Annandale

Keynes JM (2007) The general theory of employment, interest, and money, New edn. Palgrave Macmillan, Basingstoke

Klamer A (2007) Speaking of economics: how to get in the conversation. Routledge, New York

Komlos J (2014) What every economics student needs to know and doesn't get in the usual principles text. M.E. Sharpe Inc, Armonk, New York

Koopmans TC (1957) Three essays on the state of economic science. McGraw-Hill, New York

Kuhn TS (1970) The structure of scientific revolutions, 2nd edn. University of Chicago Press, Chicago

Kurien CT (1970) A theoretical approach to the Indian economy. Asia Publishing House, London

Laffont J-J, Martimort D (2001) The theory of incentives: the principal-agent model. Princeton University Press, Princeton, NJ

Lakoff G, Johnson M (2003) Metaphors we live by, 2nd ed. University of Chicago Press, Chicago, Ill

Lawson T (2003) Reorienting economics. Routledge, London

Lipsey RG, Lancaster K (1956) The general theory of second best. Rev Econ Stud 24(1):11–32

Mackay C (1995) Extraordinary popular delusions and the madness of crowds. Wordsworth Editions, Ware

Mazzucato, M. (2013). The entrepreneurial state: debunking public versus private sector myths. Anthem Press, London

Mearman A (2007) Teaching heterodox economics concepts. http://www.economicsnetwork.ac.uk/handbook/printable/heterodox.pdf
Milgram S (1974). The perils of obedience. http://isite.lps.org/jhanda/web/documents/ThePerilsofObedience-S.Milgram.pdf
Mishan EJ (1993) The costs of economic growth, Revised ed. Praeger, Westport
Murray CJL, Lopez AD (1999) On the comparable quantification of health risks: lessons from the global burden of disease study. Epidemiology 10(5):594–605
Phillips PCB (2003) Laws and limits of econometrics. Econ J 113(486):C26–C52. doi:10.1111/1468-0297.00114
Pinker S (2007) The stuff of thought: language as a window into human nature. Viking, New York
Robinson J (1970) Capital theory up to date. Can J Econ 3(2):309–317
Rosen S (1972) Keynes without gadflies. In: Hunt EK, Schwartz JG (eds) A critique of economic theory. Penguin, Harmondsworth, pp 397–419
Saxe JG (1878) The blind men and the elephant. http://www.noogenesis.com/pineapple/blind_men_elephant.html. Accessed 7 Nov 2011
Schumpeter JA (1976) Capitalism, socialism, and democracy, 5th edn. Allen and Unwin, London
Sen AK (1977) Rational Fools: A Critique of the Behavioral Foundations of Economic Theory. Philos Public Aff 6(4):317–344
Severin WJ, Tankard JW (1997) Communication theories: origins, methods, and uses in the mass media, 4th edn. Longman, New York
Smith A (2007) An inquiry into the nature and causes of the wealth of nations. Harriman House, Petersfield
Stretton H (1999) Economics: a new introduction. UNSW Press, Sydney
The Royal Swedish Academy of Sciences (2008). The Prize in Economic Sciences 2008: Information for the public. http://nobelprize.org/nobel_prizes/economics/laureates/2008/info.pdf
Tome JF (2001) Economic man vs. heterodox men: the concepts of human nature in schools of economic thought. J Socio-Econo 30(4):281–293. doi: 10.1016/s1053-5357(01)00100-7
Tullock G, Watson AS, Swan PL, Hogan W, Edwards GW, Rae PE, Brennan HG (1983) The economics of bureaucracy and statutory authorities. Centre for Independent Studies, St Leonards
Tversky A, Kahneman D (1981) The framing of decisions and the psychology of choice. Science 211(4481):453–458
Tyler TR (2000) Social justice: outcome and procedure. Int J Psychol 35(2):117–125
Weaver DH (2007) Thoughts on agenda setting, framing, and priming. J Commun 57(1):142–147
Weng W, Yang F (2014) The impact of social identity on trust in China: experimental evidence from cross-group comparisons. Appl Econo 46(16):1855–1860. doi: 10.1080/00036846.2014.887196
Williamson OE (1975) Markets and hierarchies, analysis and antitrust implications: a study in the economics of internal organization. Free Press, New York
Zimbardo PG (1999). The Stanford prison experiment. http://www.prisonexp.org/. Accessed 13 Dec 2009

Chapter 3
Logical Gaps: Path B—Theory to Empirical Formulations

Abstract Economics focuses heavily on quantitative research methods, in particular on econometrics. There are conventions that are followed in the selection of data and choice of relationships and functional forms. This is a safe way to conduct research in terms of peer acceptance. Unconventional approaches require far more justification. This chapter challenges the conventions in the choice of data by discussing aspects of aggregation, proxy variables, and indices. For functional forms, attention is given to the use of control variables, the nature of causality, including INUS conditions, and the assumption of structural stability.

Keywords Econometrics · Aggregation · Proxy variable · Control variable · Causality

I recall attending one economics conference where virtually every keynote speaker made the plea that economists should actually go out and talk to people. Unfortunately, it seems largely to have fallen on deaf ears. The heavy focus is on getting a suitable database and then simply doing the analysis through an appropriate software package. It is not even necessary to look outside the office window.

This is unfortunate. From my own experience, an outward looking approach can be very rewarding in terms of the resulting insights into both the research topic and the perspectives of a wider audience. In many cases, these other perspectives complement existing understanding and result in enriched analyses. It promotes critical assessment and serves as a reminder of the necessary but often overlooked simplifications and distortions in the methods economists use.

In contrast to this broadly based approach, econometrics is currently the primary applied economics research technique taught to students. It has reached the point where 'research methods' courses are frequently simply econometrics courses by another name. Numerous textbooks for economists focus on econometrics, and economists' research techniques have generally focused heavily on quantitative methods of analysis. Within these, the emphasis for correct application is primarily on a narrow range of standard concerns, such as autocorrelation and multicollinearity, and the use of appropriate tests and estimation methods. These are important, but when teaching econometrics, I found myself drawn to many other aspects that

S. Birks, *Rethinking Economics*, SpringerBriefs in Economics,
DOI 10.1007/978-981-287-176-3_3

can easily be overlooked. As will be discussed here, there are issues to be addressed before the quantitative analysis, and further steps once the quantitative results have been found. These aspects generally receive scant attention in the textbooks. However, they are important determinants of the practical value of the results of the analysis. Without due consideration, the analysis may appear impressive at least for some of the audience, but the status it is awarded may be inflated. Such an interpretation is presented as 'reasoning from method', one of the 'modes of argumentation' described by Dunn (2004) which relies on the status of the method, such as econometrics, to persuade the audience.

Consider the link between a theoretical formulation and an empirical formulation. Desai (1981, p. 96) has made the point that a statistical test of a theory is actually a test of both the theory and the test. A poor test could have many false positives and false negatives. In many cases, there may not be good tests. This chapter considers issues related to Path B, the transition from theory to empirical formulation. It asks whether formulations used for testing theories are likely to result in reliable tests. In particular, it focuses on (i) data problems, and (ii) problems of functional form.

3.1 Data Problems

Where established data sources exist, there may be commonly accepted applications of those data. This can be dangerous in that, by habit or convention, definitional or measurement problems may be overlooked, or the suitability of data for particular uses may not be questioned. For numerous reasons, the variables used in theories may not match the data gathered.

Many economic theories use static analysis related to either short-run or long-run structures. The focus is then on equilibria or optima. The same data have to be used to estimate both short-run and long-run models,[1] and the observations may not be of equilibria or optima.

Consider a basic supply and demand model. If price-quantity points are actually observed, can it be claimed that these are equilibria? At best, a price is known, along with the quantity that was traded over a period. Are the boundaries (spatial, temporal, and in terms of the goods or services selected) suitably defined? Did a single price prevail throughout, and have accurate sales data been provided? Was there excess demand or excess supply? A static model of a market ignores the movement through time, with people entering and exiting and trades occurring at different times. This suggests a flow, where there can be continuous change, and the

[1] The distinction in economics, being based on the assumption of values of certain elements being fixed or variable, is conceptual, not temporal. If, at the microeconomic level, there are short-run and long-run responses to a change in circumstances, and if the short run is not a fixed length of time for all situations, then according to economic theory, there will presumably be complex and variable patterns of lagged effects from any change.

information available to participants may convey little about the future. Even if there is some form of steady state which could resemble a static equilibrium, many trades could occur before this state is achieved. In reality, then, the information is limited (Birks 2014).

Even where data are accurate, their use may be inappropriate. For example, health outcome measures such as QALYs[2] are commonly discounted in health care evaluations to give a 'present value' in the same way as is done for monetary measures (Gold et al. 1996). It is not clear that the same approach can be taken in both cases, or how it should be interpreted when applied to QALYs (Birks 2006, 2009). Should it be said that a person's life expectancy at birth is 80 years, or that it is 31 'present years' discounted at 3 % per annum? Also, some index measures are constructed using ordinal measures. Consequently, they are at best ordinal themselves. However, they are frequently used in regression analyses as if they were cardinal (Birks 2007). This is problematic because there is no way of choosing between two series that maintain the same ordering, although the relative magnitudes of the observations within each series could be quite different.[3]

Three issues will be given particular attention here, namely aggregation, proxies and indices. The first subsection identifies spatial and temporal aggregation, using the latter to illustrate possible problems. Patterns of aggregation influence the groupings used in an analysis and hence the results. As a general issue, the way in which people are aggregated into groups is can shape perceptions. This has been described for artificially engineered social groupings (Hargreaves-Heap and Varoufakis 2002), or social justice (Tyler 2000). This can be observed in the way views of society have changed over the past 50 or so years with the emphasis moving from class groupings to groupings on the basis of gender and ethnicity. Aggregation is more widespread and more of a problem for analysis than is commonly understood, however.

The discussion on aggregation is followed by a subsection that considers what variables in an analysis might actually represent. Sometimes, they are assumed to represent the given variable, while at other times, they are taken to be acting as a proxy for something else. This possibility opens the door to several problems of interpretation. The third subsection questions the increasing use of variables in the form of indices.

3.1.1 Aggregation

Aggregation is well recognised in terms of macroeconomic variables, and different levels of aggregation might also be acknowledged in industry or employment

---

[2] Quality-adjusted life years. These measure years of life in one health state in terms of their equivalence in years of healthy living.

[3] As with series A, (1, 2, 3, 4, 5, 6) and series B (1, 5, 6, 20, 100, 1000).

classifications. Aggregation reduces the number of variables, and hence it also reduces the number of relationships between variables to be considered. This could be very useful if aggregates are to provide valid simplifications. For this to be the case, it is generally necessary to have homogeneity of the components of an aggregate in terms of their relationships with the other variables under consideration.[4] It is application-specific. Homogeneity is required only with respect to the functional relationships under consideration. Differing foot sizes are not important when buying tickets for a bus, but they are when buying shoes. A further requirement for simplicity of analysis would be heterogeneity between aggregates, as otherwise there would be two or more aggregates which, for the purposes of the analysis, behave identically. The number of variables could be reduced by combining further.

Aggregates are far more common than is commonly stated. One distinction commonly presented to describe the difference between macroeconomics and microeconomics is that the former is based on aggregate variables. However, even in microeconomics, there is aggregation over suppliers of goods and of heterogeneous units of factors of production such as labour. There are additional common aggregations that are almost universal and generally unstated. Think of aggregation (i) over time, which has implications for the timing of impacts of one variable on another, and (ii) over space, as with disregard for distance, assumptions about spatial market boundaries, or cross-country regressions which disregard differences in country size and hence weights by country and within-country averaging. The problems arising from spatial aggregation are more complex than those arising from aggregation over time. This is because time is unidimensional, whereas space is in two (or three) dimensions, and because spatially aggregated units can be of widely varying size. In addition, while time intervals such as months may vary in terms of say, the number of days or working days, the variation is far less than that of spatial characteristics for which it is generally unrealistic to assume an isotropic surface.

The example outlined here focuses on the issue of aggregation over time. While the economy operates in continuous time, economists use data that has been aggregated into discrete time intervals, as with daily, monthly, quarterly or annual data. Analysis then considers simultaneous, lead, or lagged relationships with these aggregate data.

Consider data for quarterly money supply and the price level. A simultaneous relationship running from money to prices could be interpreted as a change in money supply in this quarter having an effect on the price level also in this quarter. The aggregation issue results in an assumption that a money supply change will have the same effect on this quarter's price level, whether the change occurs on the first or last day of the quarter. Timing within the period is irrelevant. Conversely, it is assumed that an effect on the next quarter's price level will be quite different if a

---

[4] There is an exception to this requirement in the presumably unusual situation of constant composition of the aggregate as its size changes. Under that circumstance, a 'representative component' or constant combination of elements of the aggregate could be considered. The homogeneity requirement is not all-encompassing.

money supply change occurs on the last day of this quarter rather than the first day of the next. Consequently, the coefficient of a one period lag on quarterly data should not be interpreted as the impact to be expected 3 months after a money supply change. For a change on the first day of the previous quarter, the next quarter reflects the impact in the months 4–6 following the change. For a change on the last day of the previous quarter, the next quarter reflects the impact in the first 3 months following the change. To treat the lag coefficients as the effects to be expected in the current, next and subsequent quarters is to assume that all the money supply changes occur on the first day of the quarter and the price level variable measures the price level on the last day of each quarter. While reference may be made to a 'one-period lag' or a 'two-period lag', the actual lag is by no means so precise.

Note that this issue arises because the actual current and lagged impacts depend on the timing of an event and the lengths of the time periods over which data are aggregated. Longer intervals may ease the problem, but they would not generally eliminate it and they come at the cost of a reduced number of observations and less explanation due to averaging within observations. More generally, aggregation results in an approximate specification of the relationship, so tests based on such aggregated data may give false indications of the underlying relationship.

To go a step further, units of time may not equate to say units of business time. There are differing numbers of working days in a month, and there may be a difference between 'two working days' when they are a Tuesday and a Wednesday, or a Friday and a Monday.

So, even if there is in reality a fixed temporal relationship between cause and effect, aggregation problems can result in highly uncertain and imprecise estimates of the relationship. To illustrate this, consider the following simple problem.

First, two series, X and Y, are generated by the following steps (the data are in the Appendix):

(1) Let X be the value of a throw of a die. Take 50 observations, 1–50.
(2) Toss a coin 50 times, one for each X observation.
(3) If it comes up heads, the X value counts towards its matching Y.
(4) If it comes up tails, the X value counts towards the next period Y.

One interpretation (A) of this structure is that there is one occurrence of X each period, either at the start or the end of the period. There is a deterministic relationship between X and Y such that:

$$Y_t = X_{t-\frac{1}{2}}.$$

If X happens at the start of a period, the full impact on Y is felt in that period. If it happens at the end of a period, the full impact is felt in the next period. Which of these occurs is determined by the throw of a die. As an alternative interpretation (B), it could be considered as a model with variable lags, having a 50 % chance that the effect is felt in either of the current or the next period. In either event, both X and Y actually occur at a particular instant, not spread over time. This differs from the more complicated effect of a change such as a tax cut, where the effect on

Table 3.1 Lagged impact regression results

	β_0	β_1	β_2
Coefficient	−0.29101	0.961213	0.135912
Standard error	0.982915	0.205265	0.210735

disposable income (*X*) and any resulting impact on consumption (*Y*), say, can take some time.

In generating *Y*, it happened that 23 of the 50 *X* observations resulted in lagged impacts on *Y*. Pairwise correlations were as follows: $(X_t, Y_t) = 0.565516$; $(X_{t-1}, Y_t) = 0.06752$; $(X_t, X_{t-1}) = -0.01865$.

A regression, $Y_t = \beta_0 + \beta_1 X_t + \beta_2 X_{t-1} + \varepsilon$, was estimated. Despite interpretation A being based on a deterministic relationship between *X* and *Y*, the specification of time periods resulted in an R^2 of only 0.3259. A standard interpretation of this result might be that variations in *X* explain only 33 % of variations in *Y*. It could then be suggested that other variables and random error are responsible for the remaining variation. In other words, *X* is a poor predictor of *Y*. This is the standard rhetoric for interpreting such results.

Coefficients for the βs, and their standard errors, are given in Table 3.1. Note that the coefficient on the lagged variable is small and not statistically significant. By a conventional interpretation, it would be concluded that there is no lagged effect with this particular sample. In reality, 23 of the 50 observations actually have a lagged impact. Also, with the estimate of β_1 being significant and near to unity, it would be concluded that all the impact occurs in the same period as *X*.

This example illustrates two points. First, there are conventional ways in which econometric results are interpreted. Such interpretations are consistent with the results and so may reflect the underlying situation. However, other interpretations may also be possible. Consequently, the strength of findings may be overstated if they are interpreted simply by following the conventions. Second, one way to identify possible alternatives is to use data for which the underlying structure is known. Clearly, the results are then consistent with that particular structure. If results can be generated from one structure which would, by the conventions, be interpreted as indicating some different structure, then claims based on those approaches should be viewed with caution.

The problem in this example is not one of misspecification through an incorrect functional form (it is linear), nor one of an omitted variable.[5] Rather, it arises from incorrect aggregation over time. It shows the potential for econometrics to give false negatives simply because of aggregation within discrete time periods. Models with quarterly data do not merely require that the effects be felt within a quarter.

[5] Omitted variable bias is a paradoxical problem for economists. Theories about the economy are simplified representations of the real world. When testing or applying any theory, the aim is to include only the few most important variables, to the exclusion of others. Can it ever be assumed that there are no omitted variables? If not, then all estimates would display this bias.

They actually require the effects to be felt instantaneously if all the effects are to be observed within the same quarter as the cause. Lagged impacts inevitably result in impacts being spread inconsistently over time periods, resulting in imprecise estimates of the underlying relationships.

This presents an additional problem for economists. Not only are economic effects not instantaneous, but also microeconomic theory suggests distinct short-run and long-run adjustments, meaning that the effect of a change in a variable is likely to have a complex temporal structure.

Even for simple relationships, are lags likely to be of fixed length? Consider a few economic examples. There can be lags between an event occurring and a decision being made on a response. Petrol prices change, so people decide to get more economical cars. Some new equipment might be needed, but a decision has to be made at an infrequent committee meeting. There can then be lags between the decision and resulting action, and these lags may also vary. How long does it take to sell a house, or find a new job, or to get a tradesperson to do some work? There can be a lot of variation in the time between an event that can cause the initiation of an action and the end result.

In summary, time, and aggregation over time, are not trivial matters for economists. In addition to the distortions that arise from the simplified structure implicit in theory based on static analysis, other distortions come from aggregation of observed events over time. Given the potential problems as illustrated by the example here, care must be taken when interpreting estimates of lag structures and their significance or otherwise. There are alternative interpretations of the same results, and the conventionally accepted conclusions may not be universally valid. Cross-section data do not eliminate these problems. Rather, they are likely to exacerbate them. Given the importance of population groupings in much policy analysis, this raises serious questions about interpretation of evidence. If the limitations are not recognised, then the accuracy of the evidence is overstated and any resulting deliberation based on those findings may be flawed.

3.1.2 Proxies

Statistical models only 'explain' in terms of finding statistical associations between strings of numbers. The results depend on the numbers alone, with no regard for the specific variables underlying the numbers. Nevertheless, results are often interpreted as if the numbers represent specific, chosen phenomena. Two distinct variables with identical data series would give identical statistical results, although the economic interpretation of these results could be quite different. Moreover, the identified variable may, by chance or design, be acting as a proxy for one or more other variables which are, individually or collectively, correlated with it. The interpretation of statistical results as if they refer to specific variables depends heavily on this issue of proxies. There are additional problems of interpretation in situations where related variables are 'controlled for', as discussed in Sect. 3.2.1.

Given that the economic interpretation of results depends on the meaning ascribed to the data series, this is an important dimension for rhetoric in economics and for associated policy debate.

Sometimes, an index is used as a variable in regression so as to reduce the number of variables being considered. This is based on the concept of several variables moving together, so that a variable can be constructed that will represent them all and pick up their combined effects. An extreme approach would involve using a single indicator variable instead of a composite index. In other words, a single variable can be used to pick up the effects of several variables that are individually or in some linear combination correlated with that variable.

If a variable can be used that way, can it ever be said with any certainty that any explanatory variable in a regression is not serving that function? In other words, whenever an equation is estimated, the results may represent the impact not of the individual explanatory variables included in the equation, but of all the correlated variables and combinations of variables for which the included variables can act as a proxy.

This point can be illustrated by the use of a variable, 'mother's education'.[6] Several documents present results about the effects of education levels of mothers along with consequential policy recommendations. For example, from the World Bank Living Standards Measurement Study, Working Paper No. 123, *The Demand for Medical Care: Evidence from Urban Areas in Bolivia*:

> Our results also show that income and education are also important determinants of demand for medical care. For children, mother's education is far more influential than father's. (Ii 1995, p. ix)

Similar reasoning is found in Working Paper No. 128, *How Does Schooling of Mothers Improve Child Health? Evidence from Morocco* (Glewwe 1997, p. viii) and Working Paper No. 132, *The Role of the Private Sector in Education in Vietnam: Evidence from the Vietnam Living Standards Survey* (Glewwe and Patrinos 1998, p. ix). Elsewhere, numerous examples can be found, including: an OECD report (Morrisson 2002, p. 30); a UK Treasury document (Doney and Wroe 2006 p. 5); and a Joseph Roundtree Foundation document (Machin and McNally 2006, p. 13).

All these studies are making claims that could be used to support policy decisions. However, a Google Scholar search on ['mother's education' +proxy] provided over 2,500 results. From *Demography*:

> [W]e argue that maternal education may be a proxy for the socioeconomic status of the household as well as for characteristics of the community of residence. Hence, we consider the possibility that the observed correlation between maternal education and various markers of child health may be spurious…we demonstrate that controls for a few socio-economic variables and for community of residence substantially attenuate the maternal

[6] These examples relate to policy decisions which have economic implications, but note that the techniques and reasoning are applied for policies in relation to health and education. The concerns raised are not unique to economics.

> education/child health link. Based on these results, we argue that the relationship between maternal education and child health is considerably weaker than is commonly believed. (Desai and Alva 1998, p. 71)

As far as the computations are concerned, any variable that is included in a regression is considered as a string of numbers. Whatever the numbers actually represent is irrelevant for those processes, but it is essential for interpretation of the results for policy purposes. However, there is good reason to expect a variable to pick up the effects of other numerically related variables. Consequently, proxy variables can be used, but also may provide spurious results. As they rely solely on the numbers, there is nothing in the statistical techniques to allow an analyst to deduce whether the results represent the effects of the variable, of some other variable(s) for which it is a proxy, or pure chance. It would seem that some policy recommendations are claiming to be based on a stronger evidence base than is justified.

3.1.3 More on Indices

Indices were briefly mentioned above, but more can be said about indices in general. Consider first the construction of a price index, say the consumer price index. The process could be set out as three steps:

(1) Select the items
(2) Choose quantities (weights) for the items
(3) Add prices

Steps one and two are guided by the requirement that the items and their weights reflect a representative consumption bundle. While this would not match the consumption of every (or perhaps any) consumer, and actual consumption can change over time for a variety of reasons (such as changes in relative prices, tastes, or available products), there are criteria on which to base the decisions and against which they can be assessed. The third step involves identification of prices. These may vary over time and outlet, and consumers may shop around, so the selected prices may not match those actually paid. However, there can still be a clearly specified process to follow.

There has been a proliferation of indices used by economists in recent years. To name a few, there are the Healthy Housing Index; Financial Liberalisation Index; Index of Globalisation; Control of Corruption Index; Corruption Perceptions Index; Health Utility Index; Human Development Index; Australian Unity Wellbeing Index; and Economic Living Standards Index. For each of these, some equivalent of the above three steps must be followed.[7] To give them in a general form, the steps are:

---

[7] A related three-step procedure applies to claims of advantage or disadvantage for a chosen group. This relates more to policy and is outlined in Sect. 4.4 below.

(1) Select items
(2) Choose weights
(3) Add values

The process is described for the Economic Living Standards Index in Birks (2007). To summarise:

(1) Items for inclusion are answers to: seven questions on ownership of a telephone, washing machine, etc. (yes, or no because did not want, could not afford, or other reason); seven activities such as visit to hairdresser, friends for dinner with similar response options; eight economising measures ('spend less time on hobbies than you would like to help keep down costs', no, a little, a lot); three self-assessment well-being questions on four or five point scales. There is no clear reason for the number and choice of these items.
(2) The questions were all given equal weight.
(3) Values were then based on these responses, coded up (0 or 1 for some questions, 0–4 in integers of others, etc.) with no clear reason for these values. With the same orderings, responses to questions could have been given values 0 or 50, or 0, 1, 4, 10, and 30, say.

Given the changes to values on individual questions, or altered weightings, the ordering of index measures could be quite different. Even if the ordering were maintained, the actual index values could follow a very different pattern (exponential compared to linear, for example). This is a major concern where index measures are used as variables in regressions. As was shown in Birks (2007), changing the scaling while maintaining the ordering can result in a change not only in magnitude, but also in the sign of a regression coefficient. With no basis for preferring one scaling over another, the sign cannot be determined with any accuracy. However, policy directions are recommended on the basis of signs of coefficients. Hence a positive relationship can result in a suggestion to increase X, so as to bring about an increase in Y. Consequently, the potential to change the sign by re-specification of the values of an index variable can be very important. Of course, this problem is not generally recognised with only one representation of the index being used. It is a general problem when ordinal measures are treated as if they were cardinal, and many indices are, at best, ordinal.

There are numerous price indices because the 'representative bundle' varies according to the area of application. A specific price index only gives a rough approximation of price level changes faced by an individual or a household. Similarly with other indices, they only approximate the experience of individuals or subgroups of the population. This is important to note in a broader policy setting, as will be discussed in the next chapter.

3.2 Functional Forms

Theory generally does not give the specific form of relationship to be estimated.[8] This is clearly the case with static models, as timing and lagged effects are not considered. One simple, but powerful description of the functional form problem was presented in a seminar at Massey University several years ago by a visiting geography professor. He used the concepts of an input wave and an output wave. In a single equation model, an independent variable provides an input wave, following a particular pattern over time. There is then a resulting effect on the dependent variable, which can be described as an output wave, a particular pattern of effect over time. In a model, the relationship between the two variables is fixed by the functional form. With a linear relationship, the output wave matches the pattern of the input wave. All the regression does is estimate sign and the magnitude of the effect. This is highly restrictive, but it is a starting assumption in most estimated relationships.

It is not the only strong restriction imposed by linear models, another being additive separability. In a multivariate linear equation, a unit change in the value of any variable is assumed to be associated with a fixed change in the dependent variable irrespective of the starting values of the two variables or the values of any other variables in the equation. In many specific applications, these assumptions would seem to make no economic sense.

Two additional concerns, controlling for other factors and causality, are described here.

3.2.1 Controlling for Other Factors

A Google Scholar search for 'vector of control variables' in articles conducted on 27 February 2009 produced 'about 4,140' results. Repeated on 24 October 2012, the number had grown to 'about 8,780', and 'about 10,800' on 11 March 2014. It has become common practice to convert basic models with a few variables into ostensibly more complex and realistic models simply by adding 'control variables'. It is then claimed that the effects of those variables have been taken into account, with the results for the variables under investigation being those observed having made full allowance for the other effects.

---

[8] Even when it does, the approach has been criticised. For example, Mende (2005) suggests that researchers are too quick to move into estimation and application of quantitative techniques, thereby possibly missing numerous other possible perspectives. Similarly, Lindblom (1990) and Dunn see much standard social science policy research as being locked into established frameworks and 'little more than a ratification of conformity" (Dunn 1997, p. 277). For a broader criticism of the requirement of a stable underlying structure, "The most telling point against [econometrics is that] significant invariant event regularities...have yet to be uncovered in economics' (Lawson 1997, p. 70), and Carr (2008, p. 171) talks of history being concerned with processes of change (i.e. changing structures), while economists 'take cover' in econometrics.

Without further explanation of the functional form, this is pure rhetoric. Consider what it means in a linear regression. It has to be assumed that, for a unit change in a control variable, when the dependent variable is:

- A number—the control variable has a fixed numerical effect;
- A log—the control variable has a fixed proportionate effect;
- A total value (such as GDP)—the control variable has a fixed total effect;
- A per capita value—the control variable has a fixed per capita effect;
- A nominal value—the control variable has a fixed nominal effect;
- A real value—the control variable has a fixed real effect;
- A first difference—the control variable has a fixed effect on the first difference.

Should it be simply assumed that, whichever of these is used, it results in the relationship being correctly specified? When a researcher experiments with alternative specifications for the dependent variable, can it then be assumed that the alternative functional forms all correctly reflect the relationship with the control variables? This would appear to be highly implausible if not impossible.

As an alternative explanation of the problem, consider standard approaches to the use of data in different currencies (adjusting for exchange rate differences by converting to a common currency) or different price levels (adjusting for inflation by converting from nominal to real values). There is an economics rationale for such adjustments, even if they are imperfect. Instead of making these adjustments, would it be considered acceptable to add an exchange rate or a price index as an additional 'control' variable in a linear regression? The implication would be that the effect of say a price level change is independent of the magnitudes of all other variables. If such an approach is unacceptable, why should it be assumed sufficient when controlling for any other influences?

There are also problems of Interpretation of results where control variables are present. Control variables may sometimes be considered as a means of adjusting (in a restricted way) for aggregation problems in the data. For example, consider analysis with data on household behaviour where socioeconomic group might be important. Dummy variables could be added to allow for some difference in overall affect according to category, but it is a very specific form of adjustment (a one-off shift, irrespective of the values of other variables). In other cases, their use lends itself to an interpretation such as, 'if policies were introduced *to successfully eliminate the effects of the control variables* (such as socioeconomic status), then the relationship between the other variables may be as estimated'. An additional rejoinder is then needed, 'however, the policies do not have to be introduced', which bears a close similarity to the reasoning underpinning the Kaldor-Hicks compensation criterion.[9]

---

[9] A change is considered a Pareto improvement when at least one person gains and nobody loses. However, this does not help decide on the large number of possible changes where there are both gainers and losers. The compensation criterion asserts that, when considering such a change:

'There is no need for the economist to prove-as indeed he never could prove-that as a result of the adoption of a certain measure nobody in the community is going to suffer. In order to establish his case, it

Similar issues have been identified in psychology, especially building on the work of Urie Brofenbrenner, who recognised the impact of wider social factors on individual behaviour. As one illustration, Brofenbrenner challenged the idea that the effects of certain factors can be taken out, so as to analyse interactions between others:

> [Brofenbrenner] went on to explain that it made no sense at all to control for ethnicity, social class, or household composition in an attempt to isolate 'pure' process. No processes occur outside of a context. And if we want to understand context, we need to take it into account, not pretend to control it away. (Steinberg et al. 1995, p. 424)

This suggests a major problem with much of the quantitative work in economics. Unstated and untested assumptions are being made right at the specification stage. This will generally have an impact on the results, but not in any predictable or meaningful way. Specification error is a concern raised in econometrics textbooks, but not commonly in relation to control variables.

3.2.2 Causality

There are well-recognised causality issues, such as:

- The distinction between correlation and causation and whether a statistical relationship is actually causal at all;
- If it is causal, whether it is a relationship between two identified variables or involving some additional variable(s);
- The direction of causality between variables (one way from A to B or B to A) or two way);
- The timing of the impact.

As indicated in several examples above, these matters may be glossed over in many studies.[10] Economic analysis relies heavily on econometrics to estimate relationships between variables. The results may then be used to influence policy

---

(Footnote 9 continued)
is quite sufficient for him to show that even if all those who suffer as a result are fully compensated for their loss, the rest of the community will still be better off than before'. (Kaldor 1939, p. 550).
See also Hicks (1939).

[10] One common misunderstanding is that tests for Granger causality actually test for causality. Granger causality uses statistical tests based on a presumption of *post hoc ergo propter hoc*, the earlier occurrence causes the later event. Some treat this as a test of causality, but it is really a case of Schopenhauer's second stratagem for winning an argument, 'the homonymy', where '[the] trick is to extend a proposition to something which has little or nothing in common with the matter in question but the similarity of the word; then to refute it triumphantly, and so claim credit for having refuted the original statement' (Schopenhauer c1851, 3.II). The problem in this instance can be seen by consideration of an increase in retail spending followed by Christmas. The former is a response to the latter, despite it occurring first (This highlights an additional problem for economists, in that behaviour is based on perceptions of the environment. These may differ in substance and timing from events in the environment themselves, however, most data series are attempts to measure real rather than perceived phenomena.).

decisions. The recommendations are based on simplified assumptions about causality. The existence of more complex relationships is indicated by some recommendations that do not seem to fit very well within this framework. In Israel, a comprehensive stabilisation programme was effective using a range of policies working together, whereas traditional approaches relying on fewer policy instruments had failed (Cukierman 1988, p. 48). A combination of measures was required to achieve a health objective in African countries (James et al. 2006, p. 148). In youth smoking prevention, Ross et al. (2006) describe a range of policies used to change the whole environment, considering that their success depended on the multidimensional approach. An OECD Policy Brief mentioned above, (Morrisson 2002), refers to mothers' education and poverty. While it mentions the statistical link between mother's education and child health, and talks of a relationship between mother's education and the demand for education for children, it also talks of 'clusters of factors' and 'combinations of disadvantages'.[11]

The common feature of these examples is that individual policies might be ineffective. For successful outcomes, a package of policies is required. This is consistent with an INUS approach to causality, whereby outcomes require the coincident occurrence of a specific combination of factors, and there may be several alternative combinations that can achieve the same outcome (Addison et al. 1984).[12] Policies in isolation may be ineffective, but in the right combination they can work, and there may be several alternative approaches to choose from. To rephrase this, a policy might be effective in some situations but ineffective in others because the outcome depends on a combination of (policy and other) circumstances.[13]

This does not fit well within an econometric modelling approach because econometric models have difficulty including conditional multivariate components. Even in the relatively simple situation of binary variables (a policy is 'on' or 'off') a complex mix of dummy variables and interactive terms would be required. Take a simplified version of the first example, consider a dummy variable, D_1, equal to 1 when there is a tight monetary policy, another, D_2, for tight fiscal policy, and D_3 for a prices and incomes policy. It would then be necessary to include a variable $D_1xD_2xD_3$ to indicate a simultaneous combination of the three policies.

---

[11] Note also 'risk factors' in epidemiology.

[12] An INUS condition is **I**nsufficient on its own, but is a **N**ecessary component of a set of conditions that are **U**nnecessary but **S**ufficient for an outcome to arise. For example there are several reasons why a house might burn down (cooking fire, electrical fault, candle), but each reason is contingent on other factors (proximity of flammable material, lack of oversight, no smoke alarm, etc.). A similar point is made by Byrne and Charles Ragin using the term 'qualitative comparative analysis'. In an interview, Byrne defined this as, 'a method which is 'set theoretic', i.e. it understands causal relations in the social world in terms of relationships in combination—sets, rather than the unique contribution of single variables" (Byrne 2009).

[13] This point is central to Rodrik's case for country-specific policies, '…straightforward borrowing (or rejection) of policies without a full understanding of the context that enabled them to be successful (or led them to be failures) is a recipe for disaster' (Rodrik 2007, pp. 4–5). An entertaining description of first hand experiences of Eastern European moves to a market-driven economy can be found in Hare (2012).

If INUS conditions are included, there may be several possible alternative combinations to consider. If so, for the structure to be correctly specified, it would be necessary to include all the combinations that occurred in the sample period, set out as combinations rather than just individual variables with the outcomes conditional on one of the sets occurring. In addition to estimation problems, this suggests an additional difficulty. If the combinations of policies that can give the desired outcome are not already known, are there ways that they can be identified and/or tests undertaken to find them? This is important in a general policy dimension. A basic point is that it may be desirable to consider broad-based, multidimensional, multifaceted policy. Instead, regression approaches tend to be based on the assumption that there are individual policy variables with a fixed marginal impact on the target variables.

3.2.3 Structural Stability

Alan Greenspan's statement to the House Oversight and Government Affairs Committee on 23 October 2008 included the following:

> In recent decades, a vast risk management and pricing system has evolved, combining the best insights of mathematicians and finance experts supported by major advances in computer and communications technology. A Nobel Prize was awarded for the discovery of the pricing model that underpins much of the advance in derivates [*sic*] markets. This modern risk management paradigm held sway for decades. The whole intellectual edifice, however, collapsed in the summer of last year because the data inputted into the risk management models generally covered only the past two decades, a period of euphoria. Had instead the models been fitted more appropriately to historic periods of stress, capital requirements would have been much higher and the financial world would be in far better shape today, in my judgment. (Greenspan 2008)

This indicates a problem that can arise in understanding situations that may occur infrequently, as with some shocks,[14] or long cycles or structural changes, when people are drawing on experience only of the recent past.

A broader point is that generations each have their own experiences of the world. An older generation may make decisions in reaction to their experience of earlier issues or problems. A younger generation, observing these decisions, will not have experienced the context on which they are based. Therefore, their interpretation of their current experiences can differ from that of the older generation. A certain behaviour (or policy) could be seen as 'the way things are done', as with consumption of fast foods. Alternatively, it could be rejected as misguided or outdated behaviour of older people. This could possibly help to explain differing attitudes to debt of those who lived through the depression of the 1930s, those born after the Second World War, and those born in the 1980s.

---

[14] Taleb refers to these as 'black swans' (Taleb 2005, 2007). Winston (2005) distinguishes between perspective and analytic time, pointing out the problem for economics of unique events.

A further potential problem that Greenspan. did not mention is that, depending on the complexity of the estimation of risk of default on mortgages, the calculation may be giving the average risk of default, whereas the important measure, at least in an expanding market, would be the marginal case. Risks may be rising as more loans are given to people within a category, given that the marginal and average are not the same. A similar point can be observed in an example by Musgrave and Musgrave. They present results on returns to education, after which they state:

> …since there is considerable slack in student input (only about 50 % of students complete high school and only one-third of high school graduates proceed through college), it appears that considerable scope for increased investment in higher education still exists. (Musgrave and Musgrave 1973, p. 196)

However, the statistical result is the average return, and additional (marginal) students may have other characteristics and outcomes (even if only through changing pay by qualification as numbers of qualified change).

The average versus marginal issue has similarities with that of outliers. Should such observations be discarded as aberrations which distort statistical results, or are they valuable sources of information. A classic example of the value of outliers is that of the Broad Street pump (Hempel 2007). In 1854, a cholera outbreak produced numerous cases clustered around a pump in Broad Street, London. Dr John Snow noticed this when he plotted the deaths on a map. The connection with the pump was demonstrated more conclusively by the lack of deaths in a factory close by which did not use that water, and the death of a woman some distance away who was regularly supplied with water from the pump.[15]

The value of searching for and relying on a common structure has also been questioned, as in cases where only low R^2s are produced. Action research, often applied to education issues, aims to bring change through consideration of issues at a micro level. This is because the individual influences may be more important than the more generalised ones found through quantitative research. Egon Guba, in a foreword to Stringer's book on action research, writes:

> We have witnessed, over the past half-century or so, determined efforts to find general solutions to social problems…The cost to national economies has been prodigious, and there is precious little to show for it…It ought to be apparent by now that generalised, one-size-fits-all solutions do not work…Without intimate knowledge of local context, one cannot hope to devise solutions to local problems. *All* problems are de facto local; inquiry must be decentralised to the local context. (Stringer 2007, p. ix)

Parallels might be considered with the law, giving generalised solutions, and its implementation, through which individual circumstances may be considered. If the specific aspects are more important than the general, there is limited scope for laws themselves to address the problems. There are also lessons for the value of much economics and econometrics research in that this commonly seeks to obtain generalisable findings.

---

[15] The existence of relevant factors besides proximity to the pump suggests the existence of INUS conditions.

There is an additional consideration also. Of all the available information, only a small component is in the form of large, quantitative data series. This is particularly true with the growth of new information technologies, providing large quantities of readily accessible textual and other data along with means to quickly search and analyse them. Consequently, other approaches to research and the use of alternative types of data may give additional valuable insights into phenomena of interest to economists.

3.3 Conclusions

Data problems and limited functional forms can place significant constraints on empirical analyses. This is not entirely surprising for two reasons. First, econometrics is constrained by the restrictive nature of relationships it is used to estimate, with many potential alternatives assumed away at the initial specification stage. Second, econometric results focus on the average, or the common features, which may tell only a small part of the whole story. Nevertheless, as Dunn has suggested, as a mode of argumentation, these techniques may be persuasive. There is a strong rhetoric that surrounds them that can be difficult to challenge. This may result in decisions being based on misinformation and undue confidence in quantitative research results.

References

Addison JT, Burton J, Torrance TS (1984) Causation, social science and Sir John Hicks. Oxford Econ Papers 36(1):1–11

Birks S (2006) Discounting health effects in pharmacoeconomic evaluations: current controversies *PharmacoEconomics* 24:1273–1274 (ADIS International Limited)

Birks S (2007) A word of caution on indices. SSRN eLibrary. http://ssrn.com/paper=1080328

Birks S (2009) Some problems/assumptions in pharmacoeconomic analysis. In: Arnold RJG (ed) Pharmacoeconomics: from theory to practice. Fl CRC Press, Boca Raton, pp 133–148

Birks S (2014) Supply and demand models—the impact of framing. Real World Econ Rev 67:67–77

Byrne D (2009) Interview with David Byrne (interviewer Brian Castellani). http://sacswebsite.blogspot.co.uk/2009/05/interview-with-david-byrne.html. Accessed 26 Oct 2012

Carr EH (2008) What is history?. Penguin, Harmondsworth

Cukierman A (1988) The end of the high Israeli inflation: an experiment in heterodox stabilisation. In: Bruno M, Tella GD, Dornbusch R, Fischer S (eds) Inflation stabilization: the experience of Israel, Argentina, Brazil, Bolivia, and Mexico. MIT Press, Cambridge, pp 48–94

Desai M (1981) Testing monetarism. Pinter, London

Desai S, Alva S (1998) Maternal education and child health: is there a strong causal relationship? Demography 35(1):71–81

Doney M, Wroe M (2006) Keeping our promises: delivering education for all. http://www.dfid.gov.uk/Documents/publications/education-delivering-promises.pdf

Dunn WN (2004) Public policy analysis: an introduction, 3rd edn. Pearson Prentice Hall, Upper Saddle River

Glewwe P (1997) How does schooling of mothers improve child health? Evidence from Morocco. http://www-wds.worldbank.org/external/default/WDSContentServer/WDSP/IB/2000/02/24/000009265_3971031092438/Rendered/PDF/multi_page.pdf

Glewwe P, Patrinos HA (1998) The role of the private sector in education in vietnam: evidence from the vietnam living standards survey. http://www-wds.worldbank.org/external/default/WDSContentServer/WDSP/IB/1998/03/01/000009265_3980624090958/Rendered/PDF/multi_page.pdf

Gold MR, Siegel JE, Russell LB, Weinstein MC (eds) (1996) Cost-effectiveness in health and medicine. Oxford University Press, New York

Greenspan A (2008) Testimony to the committee of government oversight and reform, October 23. http://oversight-archive.waxman.house.gov/documents/20081023100438.pdf. Accessed 13 June 2014

Hare P (2012) Vodka and pickled cabbage: Eastern European travels of a professional economist [Kindle edition]. http://www.amazon.com/Vodka-Pickled-Cabbage-Professional-ebook/dp/B008IGP6RK/ref=tmm_kin_title_0?ie=UTF8&qid=1348057083&sr=8-1

Hargreaves-Heap S, Varoufakis Y (2002) Some experimental evidence on the evolution of discrimination, co-operation and perceptions of fairness. Econ J 112(481):679–703

Hempel S (2007) The strange case of the broad street pump: John Snow and the mystery of cholera. University of California Press, Berkeley

Hicks JR (1939) The foundations of welfare economics. Econ J 49(196):696–712. doi:10.2307/2225023

Ii M (1995) The demand for medical care: evidence from urban areas in Bolivia. http://www-wds.worldbank.org/external/default/WDSContentServer/WDSP/IB/1996/02/01/000009265_3961214182415/Rendered/PDF/multi0page.pdf

James CD, Hanson K, McPake B, Balabanova D, Gwatkin D, Hopwood I, Xu K (2006) To retain or remove user fees?: reflections on the current debate in low- and middle-income countries. Appl Health Econ Health Policy 5:137–153

Kaldor N (1939) Welfare propositions of economics and interpersonal comparisons of utility. Econ J 49(195):549–552. doi:10.2307/2224835

Lawson T (1997) Economics and reality. Routledge, London

Lindblom CE (1990) Inquiry and change: the troubled attempt to understand and shape society. Yale University Press, New Haven

Machin S, McNally S (2006) Education and child poverty: a literature review. http://www.jrf.org.uk/sites/files/jrf/9781859354773.pdf

Mende J (2005) The poverty of empiricism. Informing Sci J 8:189–210

Morrisson C (2002) Policy brief no. 19: health, education and poverty reduction. http://www.oecd.org/dataoecd/59/57/1851366.pdf

Musgrave RA, Musgrave PB (1973) Public finance in theory and practice, 2nd edn. McGraw-Hill, New York

Rodrik D (2007) One economics, many recipes: globalization, institutions, and economic growth. Princeton University Press, Princeton

Ross H, Powell LM, Bauer JE, Levy DT, Peck RM, Lee H-R (2006) Community-based youth tobacco control interventions: cost effectiveness of the full court press project. Appl Health Econ Health Policy 5:167–176

Schopenhauer A (c1851) The art of controversy. http://etext.library.adelaide.edu.au/s/schopenhauer/arthur/controversy/

Steinberg L, Darling NE, Fletcher AC (1995) Authoritative parenting and adolescent adjustment: an ecological journey. In: Moen P, Elder GH, Luscher K, Bronfenbrenner U (eds) Examining lives in context: perspectives on the ecology of human development. American Psychological Association, Washington, pp 423–466

Stringer ET (2007) Action research, 3rd edn. Sage Publications, Los Angeles

Taleb NN (2005) Fooled by randomness: the hidden role of chance in life and in the markets, 2nd edn. Random House Trade Paperbacks, New York

Taleb NN (2007) The black swan: the impact of the highly improbable. Random House, New York

Tyler TR (2000) Social justice: outcome and procedure. Int J Psychol 35(2):117–125

Winston GC (2005) Three problems with the treatment of time in economics: perspectiveness, repetitiveness, and time units. In: Winston GC, Teichgraeber RF (eds) The boundaries of economics. Cambridge University Press, Cambridge, pp 30–52

Chapter 4
Logical Gaps: Path C—Empirical Results to the Real World

Abstract There are statistical criteria which are commonly used to determine the value of empirical results. Good performance under these criteria does not necessarily imply value for policy making. The rhetoric around such results can be influential, but may not be justified. Results are frequently misinterpreted. There are problems with some of the tests, as with hypothesis testing and the fallacy of the transposed conditional. A limited range of resulting policy options is considered. Numerous standard policy questions are not addressed, including ease of change and the costs and benefits of change. A further issue, the use of data to show advantage or disadvantage, is discussed.

Keywords Econometrics · Policy · Statistical significance · Disadvantage

There is often a tenuous relationship between research and policy, with research sometimes playing little or no part in policy formulation and implementation. Researchers, especially those in universities, face a different incentive and reward structure. The peer review process of quality assurance relies on academics judging each other, and they may be far removed from the policy scene. One group of academic researchers that has been very critical of this process writes, 'peer review should be regarded as an untested process with uncertain outcomes' (Jefferson et al. 2002a, p. 2785), and:

> Given the widespread use of peer review, it is surprising that so little is known of its aims or effects… . There is also anecdotal evidence that peer review has shortcomings and may even have harmful effects. (Jefferson et al. 2002b, p. 2789)

Peer review's potential for gatekeeping has also been mentioned in Sect. 2.2.4 above.

There are several other components in the process of policy making, including political and media debate, response to pressure groups, and shaping or reacting to public opinion. Research is not necessarily directly focussed on policy, and the approaches taken by researchers do not necessarily directly address policy questions. Nevertheless, researchers sometimes describe policy implications arising from their findings, and research findings are sometimes used directly in policy-making and implementation, often selectively chosen to support preferred positions.

S. Birks, *Rethinking Economics*, SpringerBriefs in Economics,
DOI 10.1007/978-981-287-176-3_4

Findings can also influence general understanding of issues. Consequently, the role of research in the policy process is worth exploring.[1]

There are several forces at work that result in a tendency to favour simplified views of issues.[2] They can be observed at each of three 'levels of discourse' described by Desai, namely theory, data analysis and policy (Desai 1981, p. 93). At the theoretical level, there is the value judgment associated with Occam's razor whereby simpler theories are preferred over more complex ones, *ceteris paribus*.[3] At the level of data analysis there are constraints of available data, limitations of techniques and problems with degrees of freedom. Concerns about techniques used by economists, especially econometrics, have been raised by various writers, including Swann (2006) and Thurow (1983), in addition to Hendry (1980) and Desai (1981). Alternative techniques are described in Davis and Hands (2011), Swann (2006) and Allen (1978).

At the policy level, public acceptance can be important, in that case a simple message is often required (Birks 2014). People do not have the time or motivation to understand in detail complex issues which may have little direct impact on them. Any influence is likely to arise through group action, where groups promote preferred agendas. This can be observed through the importance of interest groups and in the limited range of options presented for consideration.

One aspect of simplification that is apparent at the level of public debate is the way that policy conclusions are frequently drawn from limited statistical evidence. While economists and econometricians are generally cautious about specifying policy implications arising from econometric analyses, at the level of broader debate and media coverage there are fewer reservations. This Chapter explores some of the limitations and potential opportunities for policy-relevant findings from econometrics. In particular, it considers what can and cannot be deduced as a result of an explanatory variable being found to be statistically significant. In addition, it indicates what aspects to address or questions to raise if econometricians and economists are to extend this work to the point where it may be directly applicable in policy debate.

Section 4.1 briefly considers the link between statistical findings and policy recommendations by academic and public sector researchers and through media coverage of research. Section 4.2 outlines some basic statistical considerations, while Sect. 4.3 considers issues associated with the step from statistically meaningful findings to more comprehensive policy analysis.

---

[1] For a recent contribution, see Wolf (2007).

[2] See also Birks (2007).

[3] While theoretical simplicity is commonly lauded, more complex analyses with longer equations, more advanced mathematics and/or larger data bases are also afforded high status.

4.1 Using Statistics for Policy

One channel for statistical analysis to influence policy is through public presentation of research findings. This may affect general understanding of issues, shaping public opinion and influencing political priorities. Even if the research was not intended for that purpose, it can be selectively drawn on, with the chosen framing influencing its impact. Similarly, at the public reporting stage academics are sometimes under pressure to provide dramatic findings, omitting possible qualifying comment and results can be misinterpreted. Where, attention is created for political purposes the focus may be on a specific finding. In a small economy with relatively few spokespeople and a narrow range of opinions, this can be associated with a visiting expert deliberately invited to promote a preferred perspective (as with agenda setting and framing, see Birks 2014). This is unlikely to result in high-level debate on alternative, possibly contradictory research findings.

This section uses M. Desai's structure to briefly consider the research phase and then focus on the less commonly discussed but potentially very significant media phase.

4.1.1 The Research Phase

McCloskey and Ziliak have identified problems in academic papers in the interpretation of statistical findings as having applications in policy making (McCloskey 1998; Ziliak and McCloskey 2004, 2008).[4] One of their central concerns is the weight given to statistical significance. They argue strongly that policy decisions should not be determined on the basis of statistical significance alone.[5] Most research articles, after finding a set of things that is correlated with student performance, immediately go to a section on policy conclusions. The steps between the statistical analysis and the section on policy conclusions are seldom discussed. (Hanushek 1997, p. 303).

Looking at recent issues of such economic journals as *Applied Economics*,[6] *The Review of Economic Studies, Economic Record* and *Southern Economic Journal*, few articles actually refer to policy implications. This may reflect a difference in

[4] Ziliak and McCloskey (2008) has been critically reviewed (Spanos 2008). However, the criticisms relate to proposed solutions to the problem. If anything, Spanos suggests that the problems themselves are more severe than suggested by Ziliak and McCloskey.

[5] This point has been made also in relation to policy in education:

[6] Based on their abstracts, econometrics was central to 10 of 11 articles in *Applied Economics* 39 (21), December 2007. Of these, three drew some possible implications for decisions/policy. More recent issues include papers using other techniques, including experimental economics, but the emphasis is still on quantitative research, predominantly econometrics.

focus between academic economists and economists working as policy analysts.[7] Some of the discussion papers from the Reserve Bank of New Zealand use econometric models of the macroeconomy and relate the results to policy decisions.[8] The research database of the New Zealand Ministry of Business, Innovation and Employment includes papers using a range of techniques, including heavy reliance on descriptive data analysis, surveys and qualitative research. Where econometrics is used, the policy conclusions tend to be tentative, however, as in a Ministry of Economic Development paper by Maré and Timmins (2007, p. 53) on firm productivity. Given the range of industries and firms and the number of geographically related factors that can affect productivity, caution about this study's findings is not entirely surprising. A strong statistical association would only arise if there is a fixed underlying structure that applies to highly heterogeneous units. This is unlikely to be the case. The same point could be made for many other studies using similar methodology.

This raises some interesting issues. Should economics research focus more on policy implications? Alternatively, are there institutional changes required to ensure that research results are not 'cherry-picked' or misapplied in the policy making process?

4.1.2 The Media Phase

Tentative conclusions are less commonly observed at Desai's. third level, that of the media and policy discourse. Politicians are expected to appear clear and decisive, despite all the actual uncertainties surrounding policy issues. The public want information that has a clear point to make, or, for personal interest, that relates to a need to change behaviour, presented without many complicating qualifications. This point was made by Bourdieu when he described 'fast thinkers', whom he describes as 'specialists in throw-away thinking' (Bourdieu 1998, p. 35). People who can operate in this way have quick, confident responses using commonly held beliefs that do not challenge listeners' opinions. They fulfil the role better than others who may be more controversial, or more cautious and circumspect. Russell, in his essay, 'on being open-minded', made a similar point decades before.

---

7 As a separate exercise, it may be interesting to see to what extent academic research impacts on policy decisions, and, if considered, whether the findings are correctly interpreted. Example 2 below is a case in point.

8 http://www.rbnz.govt.nz/research_and_publications/discussion_papers/2007/. Approximately 7 of the 15 papers in 2007 would fit into this category. The greater emphasis on policy implications from econometric analysis may be due to the Reserve Bank having defined objectives and a limited number of policy instruments. This to a degree constrains the range of analysis required, reducing the alternatives and associated costs and benefits to be considered. Nevertheless, none of the six discussion papers in 2013 directly relate to policy (http://www.rbnz.govt.nz/research_and_publications/discussion_papers/2013/).

He wrote of the relative ease with which one can appear intelligent by presenting the accepted position (Russell 1950, pp. 65–70). Chomsky spoke of the impossibility of presenting a contrary view, given the need for detailed supporting evidence and the time constraints of the news media (Manufacturing Consent: Noam Chomsky and the Media 1992). Journalists may also lack the specialist knowledge required to handle complex issues, and they are constrained by the nature of their media to be concise and entertaining (Birks 2008). Consequently, recommendations may be based on limited evidence and analysis, perhaps merely on a statistical association or ascribed to some designated 'expert'.[9] The following three examples indicate recommendations for policy or behaviour change based on some identified relationship between variables. They also show that this reasoning can be found in a wide range of areas, and that there are aspects to consider that much economic theory assumes away[10]:

Example 1: Alcohol and brain damage A *Dominion Post* article suggested that binge drinking 'damages brains' (Hill 2007, 5 November). Claiming that damage could even be caused by social drinking, the article included a call for an education programme and routine screening by health professionals.

Example 2: Single parenthood and childhood risk This is an example in a policy context where lack of statistical significance was used to draw policy conclusions. In paragraph 616 and footnote 299 of the New Zealand Law Commission's *Preliminary Paper 47*: *Family Court Dispute Resolution* (Law Commission 2002) there is reference to Fergusson (1998).[11] The paper is quoted in the footnote, 'Collectively, the findings suggest that single parenthood, in the absence of social or family disadvantage, is not a factor that makes a major contribution to childhood risk'.

This statement refers to a statistical finding on the significance of a variable. It is used to suggest that single parenthood may not be a concern as a significant relationship with associated childhood problems is not observed when the study controls for certain other factors.[12] The interpretation of this finding is a more complex matter. It must recognise the interconnectedness of many determining factors, such that the factors that are controlled for may be closely associated with single parenthood. It is therefore not realistic to simply treat single parenthood as being independent of these determinants. This is made clear in the published study. Hence Fergusson states:

---

[9] Note that one of Dunn's 'modes of argumentation' in policy debate is 'reasoning from authority' based on the achieved or ascribed status of the person presenting the information. (Dunn 2004, p. 395).

[10] See also NZPA and Reuters (2007, 1 November) on obesity and cancer, (Palmer 2007, 30 November) on job cancer risks, Perry (2008, 18 January) and Medical Update (2002). It may not be coincidental that so many examples are health related. The media considers reader interest and this often requires a personal angle (Hamilton 2004). The recommendations in the articles may shape perceptions, behaviour and policy.

[11] This example is discussed further in (Birks 2002).

[12] Note the discussion of control variables in Sect. 3.2.1.

> The implications of these conclusions are clearly that social programmes and policies that are likely to be most effective in addressing the needs of at-risk families and their children are likely to involve multi-compartmental approaches that have sufficient breadth and flexibility to address the wide range of social, economic, family, individual and related factors that contribute to the development of childhood problems. (Fergusson 1998, p. 172)

The Law Commission paper uses lack of statistical significance to contend that a factor is not important. The journal article presents its results with great care, but at the policy level it is selectively quoted to provide apparent support for a specific position. In fact, the impact of the factor may well be felt through other, related variables. This can happen due to more complex causal relationships, or because some variables (such as household income) are acting as a proxies for others. Where, a research exercise is based solely on the application of a technique (such as econometric estimation), such aspects of interpretation are not incorporated in the established conventions and can easily be missed.

Example 3: TV watching and attention problems A research paper published in *Pediatrics* found a link between children's television watching and attention problems some years later (Landhuis et al. 2007). On this basis, despite voicing reservations, the researchers recommended restricting children to no more than 2 h watching per day. This example is discussed in more detail in Sect. 4.3.1 below.

As a general point to draw from these examples, the information that is presented in reports of research contributes to the shaping of opinions and views on alternative issues and policies. At the very least, the news media do not always apply due caution in presenting these results. This is in part a consequence of inadequate specialist training and expertise. There may also be incentives to sensationalise.

The distortions may be widespread. Quite apart from statistical estimation and functional form problems, the information deduced from these findings may be flawed. This raises a fundamental question, how should findings be presented to generate more effective interpretation, especially for policy formation?[13] In addition, given the answer to this first question, what additional questions should be asked to more effectively address the requirements for good policy decisions?

4.2 Consideration of the Problems

A paper at a health economics conference in Auckland in November 2005 illustrates a common problem with the use of statistical results for policy purposes. To give fictitious data, imagine a prevalence of 18 % for some negative health measure for low income groups, compared to 16 % for high-income groups. This indicates a possible relationship between income and the prevalence of this problem. Does this

[13] For a discussion of the use of econometrics in law, including reservations and qualifications, see Harkrider (2005).

justify policies to improve the income of low-income groups? Quite aside from causality and the issue of the costs of the problem and the costs of alleviating the problem, income may be the wrong measure to look at. Changing income may not be effective, and even if it is, the best that could be achieved is a 2 % improvement for those on low income and no gain for those on high income. This might be considered fairly minimal in terms of addressing the problem, even though it is the type of policy inference commonly made.[14]

The following discussion will be based on a simple regression equation as it provides a useful structure for explanation. Consider a basic single equation multiple regression model where Y is a target variable of policy interest and X_1 can be affected by policy (i.e. it can serve as a 'policy instrument'):

$$Y = b_0 + b_1X_1 + b_2X_2 + \cdots + b_nX_n + u$$

Statistical analysis can give results such as a finding based on whether or not X_1 is statistically significant as a determinant of Y.[15] With a superficial assessment, it might be concluded that:

- If it is not significant, there is no relationship, so the variable can be ignored; or
- If it is significant, there is a relationship, so there can be a policy recommendation to change X_1.

In other words, there is heavy emphasis on the statistical significance of the estimate of b_1. Such reasoning is flawed. Statistical significance cannot be interpreted as answering all the questions required for deciding on policy intervention. Even if the relationship is one between a policy variable and a target variable, many aspects remain to be considered. For policy, it is important to know the magnitudes of impact, the variability of impact, the costs and possible side-effects of intervention and, ideally, alternative policy options should also be considered. The first two of these aspects are basic but often overlooked. They are briefly discussed here. A more fundamental issue relating to statistical hypothesis testing is then considered, followed by an issue of identification of options from statistical results. The second two points are addressed in Sect. 4.3.

(i) Magnitude of policy impact—if X is changed, how much change is there in Y?

Harkrider gives a good legal example of this point when he distinguishes between 'practical significance' and statistical significance:

---

[14] As described in Sect. 3.2.3 above, Stringer's justification for action research is based on the limited value of studies seeking generalised patterns such as these.

[15] There is scope to debate the criteria for determining whether results are 'statistically significant'. What does the test result actually show (noting the fallacy of the transposed conditional described in Sect. 4.2.1), and is the result categorical, giving a firm yes or no answer given choice of levels of significance? This discussion takes statistical findings as given, looking at the subsequent stage of interpretation of results for policy purposes.

> Practical significance means that the magnitude of the effect being studied is not de minimis —it is sufficiently important substantively for the court to be concerned. For example, econometric evidence in the context of a publishing merger may reveal that titles published by new entrants are 0.0001 % less profitable than titles published by existing entrants. That result may be statistically significant, but not substantively important. (Harkrider 2005, p. 15)

Similarly for policy, it could be asked whether the relationship between the variables and the available options for change in X_1 result in realistic and effective policy options. In addition to required magnitudes of change and costs of change, the apparent answer could be a result of the representation of the issue, as in the formulation of the equations that are estimated. These problems have been discussed in relation to Path B in Chap. 3.

(ii) Variability of policy impact

Often relatively little attention is given to the overall R-squared for an equation. Sometimes a relationship may be only poorly specified by the equation. A statistically significant explanatory variable may then be a small factor in the overall determination of the value of the dependent variable. Also, even though the significance of a coefficient is commonly discussed (as with the t-test results), this may not then be used to consider the possible variability of response to a policy of changing X_1. The estimated coefficient may be significantly different from zero, but the true value may still be quite different from the estimated value, and the effect of a change in X_1 on Y may also be variable across individual cases.

4.2.1 Interpretation of Statistical Significance

McCloskey and Ziliak have repeatedly identified problems in academic papers in the way that policy inferences are drawn from statistical findings. These are described in detail in Ziliak and McCloskey (2008), which includes a quote from Thomas Schelling on the back cover:

> McCloskey and Ziliak have been pushing this very elementary, very correct, very important argument through several articles over several years and for reasons I cannot fathom it is still resisted.

As Schelling states, McCloskey and Ziliak's points are elementary. Two of their central points are outlined here. They are that sample size is important and the 'fallacy of the transposed conditional'. They can both be simply illustrated.

On the first point, the impact of sample size on statistical results, consider the gender pay gap:

(1) With earnings data for one man and one woman, nothing can be said about the significance of any difference between them as nothing is known about the distribution of male and female earnings. More than one observation for each is required.

(2) With a larger sample, assumptions can be made and statistical tests undertaken on differences in average incomes.
(3) At the other extreme, if observations are available for every man and every woman in the population, the average male and female earnings can be calculated precisely. The estimate equals the true population value, the variance of the estimate is therefore zero. A difference as low as one cent is therefore statistically significant.

Hence, a finding that a gender pay gap does or does not exist depends on the sample size. However, this has nothing to do with significance for policy.

To state this point more generally, statistical results depend on the underlying situation and the test that is applied, where the test is sensitive to sample size, N. N is generally not related to the underlying situation. Consequently, policy decisions should not be determined on the basis of statistical significance alone.

There is a second criticism of the interpretation of statistical significance. It involves a problem with the conventional interpretation of null hypothesis significance tests. It has been illustrated through a class of examples that have been presented in several places (including Cohen 1994, pp. 998–999; Taleb 2005, pp. 206–207; and others described below). The examples have tended to take the following form. There is a test for some illness that picks up say 95 % of true cases. Someone gets a positive result. What is the likelihood that the person has the illness? Many assume that the answer is 95 %, but they are wrong. While only 5 % of those without the illness are expected to have positive test results, this could be a large proportion of results if many of those tested are well.

The explanation that is commonly given involves computing tables, and/or equations of conditional probabilities. These present the underlying logic, but have done little to change researchers' behaviour. Apparently, logical arguments are not necessarily very persuasive (hence the frequent use of rhetorical methods). It may be helpful to illustrate the point in the example by taking an extreme case. This reduces the detail required.

Consider a society that has such advanced technology that all coins are so well made that none of them are ever biased. Someone tosses a coin six times. Whatever side came up on the first toss is repeated for the next five tosses. The chance of such a result with an unbiased coin is $(\frac{1}{2})^5$ or about 3 %. An analyst is likely to reason that the chance of this occurring with an unbiased coin is so low that the null hypothesis of unbiasedness would be rejected, concluding that there is a high likelihood that the coin is biased. For this example, *this would be wrong every single time* that the reasoning is followed. It is known that false positives can occur, but, it cannot be determined if a positive result is a false or a true positive (e.g. biased coins in this example) without using additional information.

There is a difference between a statement that the outcome is unlikely if the coin is unbiased and a statement that, given the outcome has been observed, the coin is likely to be biased. The reasoning uses the former to claim the latter. Ziliak and McCloskey refer to this as the 'fallacy of the transposed conditional' (Ziliak and McCloskey 2008, p. 17).

As an alternative explanation of the fallacy, consider the following table where *A*–*D* are the four possible outcomes of a hypothesis test:

The 5 % significance level means that $19 \times P(A|H_0) = P(C|H_0)$. In other words, there is a 5 % probability of rejecting the null hypothesis, given that the first *column* applies. If a result is obtained such that the null hypothesis is rejected, then the validity of that decision relates to the first *row*, and situations *A* and *B*. However, it is often wrongly assumed that there is a 5 % chance of being wrong when the null hypothesis is rejected. With this fallacious interpretation, the condition has been *transposed from the column to the row*. It is wrong because the test considers no information about the situation when the null hypothesis is false. It is based solely on probabilities assuming the null hypothesis to be true, hence the fallacy and its name.

Hendry also demonstrates the importance of an awareness of the fallacy:

> If, say, 1,000 possibly lagged, non-linear functions of a set of candidate exogenous variables in a model with many breaks are checked for relevance at a significance level of 0.1 %, and all are indeed irrelevant, then on average *one* will be retained adventitiously... (Hendry 2009, p. 41)

It also appears in Gorard et al. (2002, p. 11), who then describe the 'prosecutor fallacy', giving an example of a fingerprint or DNA test:

> Prosecutors tend to use the probability of such a match (e.g. 1 in 10,000) as though it were the reverse of a probability of guilt (9,999 in 10,000). However, they have to argue also that there is no human error in the matching process, that the match signifies presence of the suspect at the crime scene, that presence at the scene necessarily entails guilt and so on. Above all, they have to demonstrate that the number of potential suspects is so small that a 1 in 10,000 chance is the equivalent of 'beyond reasonable doubt'. (Gorard et al. 2002, p. 12)

A legal example is also given by Volokh. He describes how a claim that few women make false rape claims can be misinterpreted as meaning that claims of rape are unlikely to be false (Volokh 2005).[16] There is another legal example where Robertson (2003) is critical of case law relating to Post-Traumatic Stress Disorder (PTSD). He demonstrates that it is wrong to use the point that '36 % of adult survivors of abuse suffered from PTSD', to assert that the presence of PTSD is evidence of this abuse. As he states, 'Its value as evidence cannot be assessed without a figure for similarly placed non-abused people... .'

4.2.2 Interpretation: Why Not Change the Relationship?

There is a fundamental point that is often overlooked. Even when the policy options under consideration are restricted to the relationship between X_1 and Y, the outcome

[16] Douglas Adams, in *The hitchhiker's guide to the galaxy* used the same flawed reasoning in his 'proof' of the non-existence of God (Adams et al. 1981, p. 60).

depends on both the value of X_1 and the relationship between X_1 and Y. Researchers tend to pick one of these, most commonly a change in X_1. For example, more education is statistically associated with higher earnings, and so a recommendation aimed at increased earnings could be to provide more education (a change in X_1). For some variables such an option is not available. Consider a statistical relationship between gender and earnings. As a general rule, a person's gender cannot be changed, so a policy recommendation might be for a change in the relationship between gender and earnings through regulation or through market intervention such as affirmative action on pay and/or employment. These amount to policy changes to alter b_1 rather than X_1. Surely, this option would be available when it is also possible to alter X_1. For many policy questions, both X_1 and b_1 may be variable, so both options should be available for consideration. Something may be variable in the real world although assumed fixed in a model.

A common economics textbook illustration of this point can be seen with the treatment of externalities. Consider, a market for a product with external costs of production. The standard treatment involves the addition of a 'social cost' curve which comprises marginal private cost plus marginal external cost. A tax can be imposed to move the supply curve in recognition of this external cost (Doyle 2005, p. 148; Stiglitz 1993, p. 180). Some texts describe such an equilibrium point as the social optimum or the efficient point (Gwartney et al. 2000, p. 128; Mankiw 2007, p. 206; McTaggart et al. 2003, p. 353; Sloman and Norris 2008, p. 162). The assumption for this latter claim to be true is that there is a fixed relationship between the marginal cost of the externality and the output of the good.[17] An alternative, if the option is available, would be to target the externality directly. This would acknowledge the possibility of varying the external cost at any given level of output. In other words, change the relationship between marginal social cost and output, which is analogous to a variation of b_1 (Mankiw 2007, p. 217; McTaggart et al. 2003, p. 352; Stiglitz 1993, p. 589). Even if an optimal reduction in external costs is achieved, the outcome may not be optimal overall, given that losers are not compensated.

The approach of targeting the externality directly can be taken further. In the supply and demand diagram the externality is measured not in terms of the volume, but in terms of the value of the externality associated with an additional unit of output. Policies that target the externality directly and vary the volume of the externality assume a fixed value (cost) per unit of externality. Instead, it may be possible to alter this value Coase (1960) gives the example where people who are affected by an externality could move away so as to avoid the effects, thereby reducing the costs of the externality. In other words, a reduction in an external cost can be achieved through altering output, altering the production process, or altering the behaviour of those affected by the externality. In general, there may be many

---

[17] Even that is not enough to fully internalise the externality as there is no compensation paid to the losers.

Table 4.1 The transposed conditional

	Null hypothesis true	Null hypothesis false
Reject null hypothesis, H_0	*A* (false positive)	*B*
Accept null hypothesis, H_0	*C*	*D* (false negative)

options available to alter the relationship between a variable, X_1 and another variable, *Y*.

There is an additional stage that could be added to Coase's assessment in his classic 1960 paper. His starting point is where the activities are in place. The courts then allocate property rights, after which the parties can then negotiate a mutually beneficial agreement.[18] As this discussion illustrates, and as summarised in Table 4.1, an issue can be considered in increasing detail by allowing changes in additional variables. Instead of starting with activities in place as in Coase's farming example, consider people choosing strategies on location of an activity under an existing set of rules on allocation of property rights. The rules open up the possibility of game playing, or one party threatening or actually imposing costs on another. Coase writes of a cattle-raiser expanding his activity when he would have to compensate a neighbouring crop farmer for any damage caused. He rightly suggests that this would not result in the neighbour expanding production to benefit from the compensation (assuming the crop farmer is a price taker). However, consider two cattle raisers as neighbours. If a crop farmer where to consider buying the land from one of the cattle raisers, this would impose costs on the remaining cattle raiser not directly involved in the purchase transaction. Consequently, existing rules can be used strategically (just as they can in sport, as with forcing or conceding penalties). In other words, economic analysis can become more complex, but also possibly, more realistic, through increased relaxation of *ceteris paribus* conditions. In this case, the nature of relevant law and the operation of the legal system impact on possible strategies and disputes and on the process of resolving these disputes. Further steps could relate to the interpretation of and determination of the rules. Note that these two are not the same. For example, the courts interpret existing laws, whereas politicians make or revise them. Interpretation can be changed through case law and through public campaigns to change perceptions on issues (if something is seen as important, a judge may decide to 'send a signal', for example). Laws can be changed through the political process.

---

[18] The so-called Coase Theorem asserts that, with no transaction costs, bargaining can result in an efficient outcome in the presence of externalities irrespective of the initial allocation of property rights. This was not the point that Coase was making, however. He recognised the significance of transaction costs and suggested that this might limit the negotiation. Consequently, he considered it important for efficient activity that the courts make the right allocation in the first place. This point has often been missed, as he indicated in his Nobel Prize lecture (Coase 1991), in which he objected to the interpretation by others of his findings with, 'the infamous *Coase Theorem*, named and formulated by Stigler… I tend to regard the Coase Theorem as a stepping stone on the way to an analysis of an economy with positive transaction costs'.

Table 4.2 Negative externalities, levels of intervention

Target for policy	Impact of policy
Tax on output to reflect the negative externality	Market for the good, change quantity of the good
Change the amount of externality per unit of output	Internalise the externality, change relationship with the externality
Change the impact of the externality	Changed behaviour by those affected by the externality
Change initial conditions	Strategic location decisions
Change rules 1	Rule-interpretation processes
Change rules 2	Rule-determination processes

Beyond this, there are additional aspects to consider, including process and development over time with path-dependent changes in institutions and expectations. This illustrates the limited extent of the explanation contained in the initial supply and demand depiction of the effects of externalities. It also illustrates framing in that estimated models are bounded in their assumptions as to what can be changed, thereby limiting the range of policy options considered.

Others have given detailed but highly accessible descriptions of additional aspects to consider when analysing markets. Kurien (2012) argues strongly for an approach focussing on ownership, intermediation and asymmetry of information as key concepts apply when analysing economic issues. Hare (2012) draws heavily on personal experience to highlight, in an entertaining and highly readable account, the importance of real-world considerations for economic reform in Eastern Europe (Table 4.2).

4.3 There Are Standard Policy Questions Not Covered by the Econometrics

The examples in Sect. 4.1.2 above indicate that policy conclusions may be drawn or behaviour changes suggested on the basis of statistically significant relationships between variables. This can lead to poor decisions as there are additional aspects that must be considered for a proper assessment. To illustrate, Example 3 on p. 59 is discussed here in more detail. While laws are unlikely to be drafted on the basis of this particular analysis, it illustrates the sort of thinking that may be used to justify policy interventions, and in some instances these involve legislative measures or decisions.[19]

[19] The use of law for policy, including economic policy, is an important area in itself. Elected politicians make laws, and so see this as a policy instrument. Legal processes and legal reasoning are then important for implementation. There is also rhetoric in law, described as 'judicial eloquence' by Smith (1963).

4.3.1 An Example: TV Watching and Attention Problems

In September 2007, there was media coverage of a study on childhood television viewing and attention problems (Landhuis et al. 2007). It serves as a useful illustration of the potential problems that can arise if policy recommendations are made on statistical association alone. One report in *The Press* (Hann 2007) included the sort of information contained in a media release by the researchers (Hancox 2007), together with further information from one of the researchers and a personal angle from a Christchurch mother. The main finding of the study was that children, 'who watched more than 2 h…of television per day during childhood had above-average symptoms of attention problems in adolescence' (Hancox 2007). The media release also included the claim, 'this is the first time that watching television has been linked to attention problems in adolescence'.

To put this in other words, until then there had not been any observed statistical relationship. Readers of the newspaper article might have concluded that a causal relationship had been found, although that is not the case. The published study says, 'As with any observational study, we were unable to prove that childhood television causes attention problems in adolescence' (Landhuis et al. 2007, p. 536). It also presents possible alternative explanations for the observed relationship, but reasonably suggests that there may be some causal link, and that some limiting of viewing may be prudent for heavy viewers. The study includes a recommendation, 'It, therefore, seems prudent to observe the recommendation of the American Academy of Pediatrics to limit children's television viewing to a maximum of 2 h per day' (Landhuis et al. 2007, p. 536).[20]

There are several additional questions that could have been asked. On the statistical findings, it was found that childhood television viewing was associated with adolescent attention problems with a standardised regression coefficient of 0.12 and p of 0.0001. When adolescent television viewing was added to the equation, the coefficient fell to 0.06 and p rose to 0.0515, with results for adolescent television viewing being 0.16 and $p < 0.0001$ (Landhuis et al. 2007, p. 534). If television viewing hours when young are correlated with viewing hours when older as this suggests, care should be taken in concluding that younger viewing causes problems later. It may not be possible to separately identify the effects of earlier viewing as suggested.

Questions could also be asked on the interpretation of the results in terms of recommended actions. Should the matter be a concern? What are 'attention problems'? Are they really problems, and how serious are they? How many children have these problems, and what is the actual difference associated with extra hours of television viewing? What magnitude of benefits might be expected from reducing

[20] Figure 1 of the study (Landhuis et al. 2007, p. 535) indicated fewer attention problems among those watching for 1–2 h per day compared to those watching less than 1 h per day, which suggests first that the relationship may be non-linear, and second that increased viewing may be beneficial for low watchers (if the relationship is causal).

younger children's viewing? If viewing is reduced, what would the affected children be doing otherwise (do the average results apply to all)? If there are benefits from improved attention, what other ways might there be to bring about this change? Might any of these alternatives be easier to achieve or more effective? Are there benefits from television watching that might counterbalance the costs? It would appear that there are a number of additional questions that should be considered before deciding on policy responses.

4.3.2 Policy Questions

As indicated by the example in 4.3.1, there are not only statistical issues to consider, but also a number of specific policy questions to ask when drawing policy conclusions from quantitative analyses such as multiple regression. An 'ideal'[21] economic approach to policy decisions (assuming perfect information and zero costs of analysis) involves identifying all the available policy options, determining their effects, valuing them to calculate costs and benefits, and then applying a decision rule to select the best option. A statistically significant relationship in a regression equation tells nothing about alternative options. Nor does it address the question of costs and benefits. All it demonstrates is that it may be possible to alter the value of Y by changing the value of X_1. Outstanding questions[22] include:

(a) Can you change *X*?
(b) How can *X* be changed?
(c) At what cost?
(d) How much control is there over this change (how precise are the changes in *X*)?
(e) How variable are the effects on *Y*?
(f) What lags are there?
(g) What is the *value* of the resulting change in *Y* (what is the benefit, does it outweigh the cost)?[23]
(h) Are there any distributional effects (gainers, losers)?
(i) Are there any side-effects?

[21] By this I mean a textbook 'ideal'. Note that criteria to be considered, methods of evaluation, and choice of decision rule are all open to question.

[22] While these questions are raised in relation to econometric studies, they apply to all policy options where one (policy) variable is altered so as to bring about a change in another (target) variable.

[23] This is one of the key concerns raised in Ziliak and McCloskey (2008). Note that effects on *Y*, and the policy significance of the resulting *Y*, may not always be continuous. This can cause particular problems, especially where variability of outcome is important. Consider the difference, for a non-swimmer standing in a tank of water, between a situation where the water level is exactly at shoulder height and one where the water level is, on average, at shoulder height. Econometric estimation gives average impacts only.

(j) Is it possible and desirable to change the relationship between *X* and *Y*?
(k) Are there other, more desirable policy options available?

In summary, it is important to consider the ability to change the target variable, and the costs and benefits of such a change, along with those of alternative policy options to address the same problem. This information is not provided through a t-test.

While this point may be readily understood, there is an additional dimension to consider. It illustrates a group having its own perspectives, techniques and conventions. The above questions do not fit many of the conventions and standard dimensions used by econometricians for critical assessment of econometric analyses. The same could apply to other disciplines and to professions. Each may have its own perspectives, techniques and conventions, and these may not be regularly re-evaluated. Group cultures and group beliefs that may not match those of other groups, and which may not stand up to careful scrutiny, are to be expected within disciplines, professions, and political and social groups. Collier presents a telling comment which may demonstrate a key institutional barrier to broader criticism:

> Particular Institutions and false beliefs about them may be in a *functional* relation, such that the false beliefs serve to preserve the institutions that they are about…to propound the truth is not just to criticise, but to undermine the institution. (Collier 1994, p. 172)

4.4 An Additional Example: Advantage and Disadvantage

> Inequality measures relatedness. A statement about inequality must be embedded in a context within which comparison becomes meaningful. (Macdonald and Spruyt 2014, p. 103)

A common feature of policy debate is the discussion of whether chosen groups are advantaged or disadvantaged. Such claims can be analysed using a similar structure to the one described in relation to indices in Sect. 3.1.3 above. To show advantage or disadvantage, three steps are required:

(1) Define groups for comparison;
(2) Choose a measure for which values vary over groups;
(3) Interpret differences as advantage or disadvantage for the chosen group.

The three steps in construction of indices can be used as a basis for critically assessing the meaning and applicability of an index. Similarly, the above three steps can be used to look critically at any claims of advantage or disadvantage. Needless to say, given the reasons for wanting to show advantage or disadvantage, any real-world examples that I use will be politically sensitive. Common ones today might relate to gender or ethnicity. Fifty years ago class distinctions or a division between capital and labour might have been more common. It may become so again with the publicity surrounding Piketty (2014). In an attempt to retain attention on the broader issues, it may be helpful to use a politically neutral example (i.e. one currently without 'traction'), such as height or age. Let's consider the three steps applied to age.

First, choose the groupings. This can be a highly political act. The chosen framing sets up an 'us and them' scenario. This is despite wide variations in circumstances often occurring within groups along with large overlaps across groups even when group averages differ. The elderly could be compared with the rest of the population, or with the rest of the adult population. The elderly could consist of those over 65, or over 75. The choice could make a big difference to the results. This is an aggregation issue, as groups will be represented by some average measure. Hence, if it is desired to have a policy shift favouring those in their late 60s, they could be grouped together with those 70 and above, for example. This highlights the possibility of large overlaps across groups, even where group averages differ.

Then choose the measure(s). Note that comparisons would differ according to which is used out of income, wealth, home ownership, income from paid work, hours worked, health expenditure, benefits received, savings out of income, number of dependents, education levels, overseas trips, sporting activity, computer literacy, food consumption, sick days per year and so on. Should individual incomes be used, or should there be consideration of intra-family transfers, household or family income and the number of dependents? Should wealth be considered along with income? Should current and future entitlements such as state benefits and inheritances be included? Are material measures the right ones to use, or are there other dimensions of wellbeing (social inclusion, family connectedness, freedom from crime and abuse)? If elder abuse is the concern, which data would be most suitable, police data on incidents or offences, or justice data on charges or convictions, or survey data? Each will give a different picture.

Given the chosen measure(s), there is then the interpretation of differences. Does lower average income of older people indicate disadvantage, or should the focus be on transfers from younger to older people? Is the health difference an indication of disadvantage for the elderly, or are they actually advantaged and overly supported by the health services after 'controlling for' age-related health differences? Are working age people disadvantaged by putting in many more working hours per week, or are they advantaged by having higher income from work (should the focus be on effort or reward)?

These points do not mean that assessments of advantage and disadvantage are of no use. They are important for any decision making in that this involves comparison of the desirability of available options. The points do highlight the nature of the framing underpinning the comparisons, however. Consequently they can be used to critically assess the decisions and perhaps to identify what would otherwise be 'unanticipated consequences'.

It is inevitable that analyses are based on groupings, if only as a result of the constraints of classifications through the use of language and the nature of quantitative data. There is a danger that this leads to a heavy reliance on these measures. There is increasing use of them as performance indicators whereby the objective is to improve those indicators even when this may conflict with broader, but more nebulous, aims of policy.

In summary, comparisons over groups are an important component of the rhetoric of policy debate. They have implications for the choice and implementation of policies. They are central components of the framing that shapes perceptions of society and the world. They influence the issues that are seen and not seen, and the values that are placed on those issues. Quantitative analyses commonly accept the available measures as the data that are available and suitable for the techniques of analysis. A more pluralist perspective would involve critical assessment of the concepts and construction of the measures, recognising additional reserves, qualifications and adjustments that must be made when attempting to use findings to make real-world decisions.

4.5 Conclusions

This Chapter has shown that there is a large rhetorical component in the application to real-world issues of results from analyses such as those using econometric models.

At the policy stage, type C errors may arise for those who go straight from quantitative analyses to policy recommendations. This is due in part to problems in the nature of statistical tests and the interpretation of the results. The criterion commonly used in statistical tests has been questioned, especially in terms of misinterpretation of results due to the fallacy of the transposed conditional. A bigger difficulty is the limited value of econometric results for addressing many of the questions which economists might wish to ask when considering choice of policy options. The results from regression models provide estimates of specified relationships between the chosen variables. If relationships are properly specified, this provides part of the information required for a subset of policy options. It is part of the information because it does not consider aspects such as the changes that can be achieved, the cost and value of those changes, and alternative policy options. It is a subset of policy options because the focus is on changing variables, not relationships, to achieve the outcomes, and the search is for common determinants that might be widely effective, while policies more closely focussed on individual circumstances are not considered. Economic analysis is commonly tightly structured within a theoretical framework. While that can be very helpful, it means that certain aspects are excluded or assumed away.

While many analysts may present their findings carefully, there is also the danger that others, including the media and the public, will draw false inferences from the results. They could also be misused in a political environment, as suggested by Dunn's argumentation by method (See Sect. 3 of Birks 2014). Consideration of these factors and attention to the additional issues could increase the value of econometric analyses by placing them in a wider analytical context. Recognition of the issues also results in an additional range of research questions, types of data and associated research methods, that economists could profitably consider.

Even where comparisons of outcomes or comparisons over groups are used to present a structured evaluation, there are potential distortions that arise from the framing of the assessments. It can be helpful, although perhaps not so politically acceptable, to critically consider the measures used.

References

Adams D, Moore S, Jones S, Jones P, Moore R (1981) The hitch-hiker's guide to the galaxy. Music for Pleasure, Ontario

Allen TH (1978) New methods in social science research: policy sciences and futures research. Praeger, New York

Birks S (2002) Submission to the law commission on preliminary paper 47: family court dispute resolution. http://econ.massey.ac.nz/cppe/issues/LCPP47sub.htm. Accessed 7 Jan 2008

Birks S (2007) To KISS or not to KISS. Asymmetric Inf 11–12 (28 March). http://www.nzae.org.nz/news/newsletters/AINo28-March2007.pdf

Birks S (2008) The media and an informed electorate—an economist's perspective. Paper presented at the power & place: refereed proceedings of the Australian & New Zealand communication association conference, July 9–11, Wellington. http://www.massey.ac.nz/?aaac11238s

Birks S (2014) Rethinking economics: downs with traction. World Econ Rev 3:37–52. http://wer.worldeconomicsassociation.org/files/WEA-WER-3-Birks.pdf

Bourdieu P (1998) On television (trans: Ferguson PP). New Press, New York

Coase RH (1960) The problem of social cost. J Law Econ 3:1–44

Coase RH (1991) The institutional structure of production—Nobel Prize lecture. http://nobelprize.org/nobel_prizes/economics/laureates/1991/coase-lecture.html. Accessed 21 Oct 2013

Cohen J (1994) The earth is round ($p < 0.05$). Am Psychol 49(12):997–1003

Collier A (1994) Critical realism: an introduction to Roy Bhaskar's philosophy. Verso, London

Davis JB, Hands DW (eds) (2011) The Elgar companion to recent economic methodology. Edward Elgar, Cheltenham

Desai M (1981) Testing monetarism. Pinter, London

Doyle E (2005) The economic system. Wiley, Chichester

Dunn WN (2004) Public policy analysis: an introduction, 3rd edn. Pearson Prentice Hall, Upper Saddle River

Fergusson DM (1998) The Christchurch health and development study: an overview and some key findings. Soc Policy J NZ 10:154–176

Gorard S, Prandy K, Roberts K (2002) An introduction to the simple role of numbers in social science research (ESRC Occasional Paper Series, Paper 53). http://www.tlrp.org/rcbn/capacity/Papers/roleofnumbers.pdf

Gwartney JD, Stroup RL, Sobel RS (2000) Economics: private and public choice, 9th edn. Dryden, Fort Worth

Hamilton JT (2004) All the news that's fit to sell: how the market transforms information into news. Princeton University Press, Princeton

Hancox RJ (2007) Childhood TV viewing linked to teenage attention problems, Media release, 4 September, Dunedin School of Medicine, Department of Preventive and Social Medicine. http://dunedinstudy.otago.ac.nz/Publications%20and%20Documents/Summary%20and%20Media%20Sheets/TV%20attention%20FINAL.pdf

Hann A (2007) TV linked to teen attention problems. The Press. http://www.stuff.co.nz/4190202a7144.html

Hanushek EA (1997) Outcomes, incentives, and beliefs: reflections on analysis of the economics of schools. Educ Eval Policy Anal 19(4):301–308

Hare P (2012) Vodka and pickled cabbage: Eastern European travels of a professional economist [Kindle edition]. http://www.amazon.com/Vodka-Pickled-Cabbage-Professional-ebook/dp/B008IGP6RK/ref=tmm_kin_title_0?ie=UTF8&qid=1348057083&sr=8-1

Harkrider J (ed) (2005) Econometrics: legal, practical, and technical issues. American Bar Association, Chicago

Hendry DF (1980) Econometrics—alchemy or science? Economica 47(188):387–406

Hendry DF (2009) The methodology of empirical econometric modelling: applied econometrics through the looking-glass. In: Mills TC, Patterson K (eds) Palgrave handbook of econometrics (vol 2: Applied Econometrics, Chapter 1, pp 3–67). Palgrave Macmillan, Basingstoke

Hill R (2007) Binge drinking 'damages brains'. The Dominion Post. http://www.stuff.co.nz/4261574a20475.html

Jefferson T, Alderson P, Wager E, Davidoff F (2002a) Effects of editorial peer review: a systematic review. J Am Med Assoc 287(21):2784–2786

Jefferson T, Wager E, Davidoff F (2002b) Measuring the quality of editorial peer review. J Am Med Assoc 287(21):2786–2790

Kurien CT (2012) Wealth and illfare: an expedition into real life economics. Books for Change, Bangalore

Landhuis CE, Poulton R, Welch D, Hancox RJ (2007) Does childhood television viewing lead to attention problems in adolescence? Results from a prospective longitudinal study. Pediatrics 120(3):532–537

Law Commission (2002) Preliminary paper 47: family court dispute resolution. http://www.lawcom.govt.nz/UploadFiles/Publications/Publication_87_207_PP47.pdf

Macdonald G, Spruyt D (2014) Aboriginal inequality: the seemingly intractible? In: Schroeder SK, Chester L (eds) Challenging the orthodoxy: reflections on Frank Stilwell's contribution to political economy. Springer, Berlin, pp 101–127

Mankiw NG (2007) Essentials of economics, 4th edn. Thomson, Mason

Manufacturing Consent: Noam Chomsky and the Media (1992) [videorecording]: Necessary illusions in co-production with the National Film Board of Canada

Maré DC, Timmins J (2007) Geographic concentration and firm productivity. http://www.med.govt.nz/about-us/publications/publications-by-topic/occasional-papers/2007/07-01-pdf/

McCloskey DN (1998) The rhetoric of economics, 2nd edn. University of Wisconsin Press, Madison

McTaggart D, Findlay C, Parkin M (2003) Economics, 4th edn. Pearson Education, Frenchs Forest

Medical Update (2002) Smoke screen. Reader's Dig (NZ Ed) 161:19

Palmer R (2007) Cancer study uncovers job risks. The Dominion Post. http://www.stuff.co.nz/4297221a19716.html

Perry M (2008) Solariums found to raise skin cancer risk in young. NZ Herald. http://www.nzherald.co.nz/section/story.cfm?c_id=204&objectid=10487507

Piketty T (2014) Capital in the twenty-first century. The Belknap Press of Harvard University Press, Cambridge Mass

NZPA and Reuters (2007) Obesity, inactivity 'strongly linked to cancer'. Stuff. http://www.stuff.co.nz/4257962a20475.html

Robertson B (2003) Evidence. NZ Law J 252

Russell B (1950) Unpopular essays. Simon and Schuster, New York

Sloman, J, Norris K (2008) Principles of economics, 2nd edn. Pearson Education Australia, Frenchs Forest

Smith A (1963) Lectures on rhetoric and belles letters: delivered in the University of Glasgow by Adam Smith, reported by a student in 1762–63. Nelson, London

Spanos A (2008) Review of Stephen T. Ziliak and Deirdre N. McCloskey's The cult of statistical significance: how the standard error costs us jobs, justice, and lives. Erasmus J Philos Econ 1(1): 154–164

Stiglitz JE (1993) Economics. Norton, New York

Swann GMP (2006) Putting econometrics in its place: a new direction in applied economics. Edward Elgar, Cheltenham

Taleb NN (2005) Fooled by randomness: the hidden role of chance in life and in the markets, 2nd edn. Random House Trade Paperbacks, New York

Thurow LC (1983) Dangerous currents: the state of economics. Oxford University Press, Oxford

Volokh E (2005) Research on false rape reports. http://volokh.com/posts/1113597035.shtml. Accessed 15 Dec 2008

Wolf A (2007) Misleading statistical studies. Policy Q 3(4):22–29

Ziliak ST, McCloskey DN (2004) Size matters: the standard error of regressions in the American economic review. J Soc Econ 33(5):527–546

Ziliak ST, McCloskey DN (2008) The cult of statistical significance: how the standard error costs us jobs, justice, and lives. University of Michigan Press, Ann Arbor

Chapter 5
A Way Forward

Abstract There is a positive message to be taken from the previous chapters. It is important not to overstate the applicability of theoretical and research findings. By placing them in context, their strengths and limitations can be identified. There is a large body of existing knowledge which, with care, can be usefully applied. The perspectives presented in the book suggest ways in which alternative schools of thought and various concept sand findings can be used in combination to provide nuanced insights. Additional questions can be raised and answered to further extend the value of research for real world policy and decision making. Such an approach can also facilitate cross-disciplinary interaction and a more inclusive approach for applied economics.

Keywords Research · Efficiency · Conventions

Consider the analogy of LEGO to represent an aspect of mainstream economics as it is currently presented. Although initially LEGO was a collection of building blocks, it is now sold in sets designed to construct specific items. The pieces fit together to form a whole, as with the mediaeval market in the Fig. 5.1.

Similarly, mainstream economics is presented as an interconnected set of ideas/assumptions/constructs which forms a unified whole. This is then often taken to be a description of the real world. As with LEGO, the overall structure is not an accurate representation of all aspects of the object. Some parts are essential, and if they are removed the structure may fall over. However, some parts are not essential for this structure to still resemble the intended object, and many of the individual pieces may be useful in the construction of other structures.

This analogy suggests that a perspective of economic theory as monolithic is restrictive and gives an imprecise representation of the real world. It also suggests that there may be many useful building blocks (concepts, theories, models) that can be useful in other ways. They could be applied on their own or in different combinations and with other components from outside the discipline to suggest additional insights. There are still additional reserves, qualifications and adjustments to be considered when conducting these applications. This perspective provides some interesting possibilities for economics research. I illustrate this with the following

S. Birks, *Rethinking Economics*, SpringerBriefs in Economics,
DOI 10.1007/978-981-287-176-3_5

Fig. 5.1 Mediaeval market.
Source: InSapphoWeTrust, https://www.flickr.com/people/56619626@N05

example, where the concept of a production function is applied to the issue of economics research.

5.1 Example: Efficiency in Economics Research

I have argued in this book that formal analyses are not representations of the real world and do not cover all the issues to be addressed. This might mean that additional informal assessment is required. It might also mean that there can be value in less formal approaches. Economics concepts can be used in a general way to construct analogous representations which may provide insights that are relevant for the real world. Here, I use a concept as a general guide to thought rather than for formal theorising or modelling.[1]

The basic idea of a production function is that 'outputs are a function of inputs'. Inputs are combined through a production process to create outputs. When economists undertake research, they are converting inputs (their labour, data, capital

[1] In an alternative informal approach Kurien (2012) uses what he terms 'thought experiments' to build up an insightful interpretation of markets.

equipment such as computers) into outputs (research findings, conference, journal and other publications). There are some simple and very general points that can be made even with an elementary analysis. The efficiency of production will depend on (i) what is being produced, and (ii) the choice of production method from the available options.

A production function specifies a relationship between inputs and outputs, where output in a period of time is assumed to be a function of quantities of inputs, commonly capital and labour, applied over that period of time. The functional relationship reflects the quality of inputs and the state of technology that is being used. The production decision for any given output and production function involves choosing a combination of inputs for the given technology. The production function can change to reflect new options as additional technologies become available. The choice of the input combination depends on technology and the prices of the inputs. The volume of output may also take into account the value of the item produced. Where marginality is assumed, there is an expectation of substitutability and infinite divisibility. Optimal quantities of outputs and inputs would meet conditions of marginal cost being equal to marginal benefit for the last unit produced and for the last unit of each factor applied. Marginalism also means that small changes in conditions will generally result in small changes in optimal combinations.

Of course, while marginality assumptions are common in theoretical representations, they do not necessarily apply in the real world. This would be readily apparent to a researcher who is familiar with the production process in question. Consequently, research-active economists are likely to already see some limitations in this line of enquiry. By extension, they should also see limitations in the application of production functions more generally.

Nevertheless, the standard findings may give some general indication of what to expect in the real world in terms of possible directions of change. Hence there are certain basic findings that could be considered. If the price of an input falls, it is likely that more of it will be used. If new inputs or production technologies become available, there is then a wider range of possible production methods and products. In response, if the aim is to be efficient, changes are likely in the way a good or service is produced and perhaps the products that are produced. If there is a change in the relative price of inputs, and if suitable technologies are available, it will be more efficient to change the ratio of inputs by substituting the inputs that have become relatively cheaper for the relatively dearer ones. If there is a new production technology, new options become available. It may well be advantageous to take up some of these options.

So what changes might arise in the research environment? Are there changes in the inputs that are available, in the costs of those inputs, and in the technologies that can be applied? If there are, then at least if marginalism and associated adjustments are applicable (and perhaps otherwise), efficiency suggests that there should be some change in the production of research. Even where there are limited production options, some changes are likely. Where these changes do not happen, it suggests that research is not being efficiently conducted. Economists might then be expected to suggest a reason such as institutional rigidities, further contending that it is a sign of lack of competition.

Some changes in the environment can be readily observed. First, consider the nature of data. For many, economics research is seen as the estimation of a model, conducting an experiment, perhaps undertaking a survey. The research is essentially the application of a technique. By this approach, data requirements are set by requirements of the technique. Mainstream economics emphasises quantitative research, and so data are commonly thought of as numerical. However, data are not just numbers or series of numbers.

A broader definition would consider all potentially relevant information as data. There are qualitative as well as quantitative data. There are interviews, academic documents, policy documents, policy debates, news media reports, images, objects and so on. Through the Internet, a vast quantity of information from all over the world is now readily available. The cost of obtaining that information is far less than it ever was before, both in time and in money. Electronic storage of textual information, along with word processing and word search technology, has resulted in greatly increased ability to process that form of information. So there have been changes in the availability of resources and in the cost of analysing those resources.

It might be suggested that the change is not providing the 'right' information for use, but this cannot simply be assumed. An approach in which research is seen as being the application of a technique implicitly constrains the types of suitable information irrespective of availability and cost. A production function analogy highlights a problem with this attitude. If economists were to consider this situation for the production of some other goods in a competitive environment, they might contend that alternatives, perhaps close substitutes, could arise. Users of these alternatives would then drive the inflexible, and hence less competitive, producers out of business. Academics are providing products primarily for the journal 'market', with selection based on peer review. Criteria for such selection are determined within the group of researchers, such that peer review is not an impartial process. With changing evaluation criteria, peer review may not be the most effective filtering or incentive mechanism, especially where changes are large.

There has also been change in relation to numerical data, as is evident in terms of availability, cost and ease of processing. This might suggest that the costs of information have fallen cross the board. However, the change for qualitative data in recent years is likely to be more significant simply because of the magnitude of the change from a low base. Much of the policy information would not have been readily available to academic researchers in the past, especially in relation to information from other countries. The availability of textual data in electronic form means that large volumes of data can be accessed and word-searched very rapidly, Internet search engines can perform global searches for words and phrases in fractions of a second. Similar documents or sections of documents can be compared almost at the click of a button, and textual data manipulation and storage can be done in ways not even imagined 30 years ago.

However, in terms of the perceived value of outputs, quantitative research may have an advantage. Outlets for publication and volume of citations currently favour quantitative research, and this has become particularly important in an environment of research assessment exercises linked to staff appointments and promotions and to university funding.

Except in terms of the feasibility of the research, therefore, data availability has little influence on economics research itself. By default, commonly data are selected to meet the requirements of a specific model, all other available information being ignored. From an efficiency of research perspective, it could be asked why no consideration is given to the use of other available data that are relevant to the issues to be investigated. How can the researcher justify not using these other data? The answer probably lies in the institutional structures and incentives faced by economics researchers.

Consideration of these factors could lead to a different perception of the process of research. As with research in general, the selection of questions to ask can be as important as the process of answering those questions. Setting the questions also frames the issues and determines what is seen.

This example has illustrated the application of the concept of a production function in a general, informal way. As a conceptual structure or representation, it is a tool which provides important insights into an issue. Moreover, as with any application, we should be aware of its requirements and limitations. Concerns such as the following may be relevant whenever production functions are used in an analysis:

1. Unlike the case of large scale production of a homogeneous product, heterogeneity is an important determinant of value in output from research.
2. Where the skill of the researcher is important or value is placed on novel data bases, heterogeneity is also observed with inputs.
3. There are different approaches needed for the various types of data, so the production processes and outputs are not homogeneous.
4. The end result of research is more evocative of a composite good with many separate components brought together to make a completed product.
5. There is uncertainty about the nature and quality of the output, and this can persist even after the production is complete (note the concept of 'credence goods', Dulleck and Kerschbamer 2006).

The production function analogy is therefore not a precise and complete representation. However, it can give useful insights. When applied as above to the issue of research in economics, it can raise questions about the nature of that research as commonly taught and conducted. It indicates alternative directions and suggests a reassessment of prevailing directions. More generally, the example suggests that economic concepts can be applied to raise questions and suggest answers. It can be useful, but it must not be forgotten that with this, as for any analysis, what is seen depends on the way the issues are framed. There are many possible frames, and they are all simplified representations, or analogies.

5.2 A Broader Context

There were two factors motivating me to consider the particular example above. They relate to the question and to the approach. First, it is a relatively under-explored area. While economists frequently undertake research to find ways in which other people can improve their position through increased efficiency, it is less common for economists to look at themselves in the same way. There are many incentives for economists to look outwards, including accepted conventions, opportunities for publication and promotion, and research funding. Inward looking critical assessments are less likely to be well received and may give scant rewards to those undertaking them. However, economists use resources to produce services so the topic merits attention.

Second, the example shows that an informal approach can be useful. Rather than mechanical application of models or techniques, economists can use the structures of economic theory as conceptual depictions for application in a range of areas. This can be considered as a way of *framing* the issue and hence it provides a particular perspective which, hopefully, will give some useful insights.

The teaching of economics has been transformed in recent years, with standardised textbooks packaged together with study guides, instructors' notes, powerpoint presentations, online test banks and so on. This has also resulted changes in content to better match the modes of delivery. The increased use of multiple choice questions requires both a preference for clear right or wrong answers and a modification of more nuanced material to fit a right-or-wrong assessment structure. In contrast, consider the style of Smith (2007), Marshall (1920) and Keynes (2007). Such classics rely far more on verbal description and careful, nuanced consideration of real world observations.

In any event, whether or not a researcher uses formal models, there is still much scope for additional deliberation and discussion to place findings in context and to consider some of the aspects assumed away in formal analysis.

To summarise, too much is read into the results of standard model-based analyses. They use a limited amount of the available information and rely heavily on questionable techniques and conventions of interpretation. They could be of far more value if seen as a component of a much wider investigation which draws in other information and pays more attention to the strengths and weaknesses of the approaches.

Two additional broad points are worth noting. First, while mainstream economics relies heavily on a theoretical world consisting solely of some defined ideal economy and associated 'market failures', in reality there is a complex mix of economic, political, social, environmental and other forces. These interact with each other and all display flaws of various kinds.

Second, at any one time there can be a complex mix of actors in a system. They may have differing objectives and diverse views of the world. Theories and models have yet to be developed which go far in incorporating such behavioural diversity within a single model.

5.3 In a Nutshell

A standard economics education consists of a collection of courses based on a selection from a limited number of established textbooks and associated study, instruction and assessment material, combined with some exposure to econometric methods. The focus is on learning the theories and methods so that the student can then understand or engage in research that follows the conventions of these bodies of literature.

There is a heavy emphasis on 'mainstream', essentially neoclassical, economics. Pluralists will argue, and can make a strong case, for a broader coverage of perspectives, inclusion of economic history and the history of economic thought and perhaps perspectives from other disciplines such as politics and sociology. While this position is implicitly supported by the material in this book, the focus here has been at one step removed from debate on competing theories. The concern has been for the rhetoric and framing that underpins the prevailing conventions. This suggests a distinct framing as described in this book. This framing highlights three areas, arising from paths A, B and C, where an analysis could benefit from critical assessment. In doing so, it raises questions which are relevant for many applications of theory and applied research where the aim is to provide relevant policy advice.

An understanding of framing and rhetoric is useful for identifying possible explanations for the existence and ongoing prevalence of the problems highlighted by these questions. Given that all exposition involves both rhetoric and framing, it also suggests ways in which the situation can be improved, not least by recognition of the nature of the problem.

The three areas refer to the relationship between theory and the real world, theory and empirical analysis, and the results of empirical analysis and identification of real world effects. It is argued that there are important aspects of each of these which can benefit from more explicit consideration than they generally receive. The points raised provide a basis for telling critiques of much of the accepted thinking in economics.

The first path is from theory to the real world. Theories, it is hoped, may bear some relationship to aspects of real world phenomena. People (and disciplines or schools within disciplines) often invest heavily in their preferred theories, claiming more from them than in warranted. The rhetoric of debate on acceptance or rejection of a theory often relies on flawed logic. An adopted position may be based solely on faith, perhaps arising from the focus of someone's education and membership of an adherent group. This might explain the focus in mainstream economics on the desirability of perfect competition and the resulting use of 'market failure' as a justification for policy intervention. However, these phenomena are not the real world, they are simplified abstractions, alternative representations. Consequently, they can be no more than analogies. As with any analogy, they may be useful in some situations, but not in others, and there are likely to be other important aspects to the real world that are not considered in the theory.

The second path arises with attempts to estimate relationships using real world data. These data may not match the variables in the theory, and, in any event, they are aggregated according to prevailing classifications. Such aggregation further limits the precision with which theoretical relationships can be specified. Two common forms of aggregation relate to time and space. The rhetoric whereby regression results are interpreted suggests a lack of understanding of these limitations, as discussed in some detail in relation to time.

Statistical criteria are based on relationships between series of numbers. Results can depend on sample size, even when this is of no importance for the relationship being estimated. Results do not depend on the variables that the numbers represent, although this is the primary reason for the relationships being estimated. Interpretation of results is often based on the named variables, although sometimes such variables are reinterpreted as being proxies for something else. The distinction is arbitrary, and there is always the possibility that results reflect other (statistically related) factors. Concerns could be raised about the accuracy and meaning of virtually any variables, but it is worrying to see the increasing use of indices. Many of these are constructed in an arbitrary fashion and are, at best, ordinal in nature. Nevertheless, novel index measures are increasingly being used as if they are cardinal and accurately reflect the intended phenomenon.

Variables are then combined in accepted functional forms, although there may be little justification for these. Conventions on the use of control variables would appear to have little if any justification, in which case they simply serve as arbitrary distortions to the estimated relationships. The nature of causal relationships is such that they may not be well specified in the relationships that are used. This is readily apparent with INUS conditions. Too much reliance may also be placed on an assumption that all observations are of the same underlying structure, and that structure is correctly specified by the chosen functional forms. A particular problem for economists might be the widespread use of estimation techniques which are based on average relationships, whereas optimising decisions in theory often depend on marginal conditions.

The third path is where decisions on policy might be made. Statistical significance is widely viewed as one of the most important criteria, if not the overriding criterion, for making policy recommendations on the basis of econometric analyses. This view persists despite repeated attempts to warn about its misinterpretation according to the fallacy of the transposed conditional.

Economic theory suggests numerous questions on feasibility and desirability of alternative policies, including the magnitude and timing of effects and the relative costs and benefits of the alternatives. Econometric analyses can help to answer these questions, but they are inadequate on their own.

Data are far broader than the numerical series required for econometric analysis. They include any sources of relevant information, including historical and current, textual and audiovisual. There is now greatly increased access to a large volume of policy and other documents from around the world. These can be of great value, and are likely to be drawn on increasingly to provide an additional component of research.

5.4 And a Final Word

There are two commonly used expressions among my colleagues, 'jumping through hoops' and 'ticking boxes'. They refer to the expectations placed on academics and the mechanistic and detached incentive systems that increasingly shape the academic environment. In this short book, I have attempted to indicate and illustrate the wide range of opportunities that exist for critical assessment of current knowledge and its application. I hope that I have also provided some constructive suggestions for economists who wish to challenge some of the established conventions. It can be a rewarding task, but it has its risks. It is encouraging to see a growing momentum for change among younger economists in particular. Progress can occur, and the path made easier, when there is wider acceptance of alternatives. An ongoing theme of the preceding chapters is the importance of persuasion. As described in Sect. 1.2.1, Cobb and Ross suggest that, at the political level, it is not enough that there is an 'identification group' that is aware of the need for change. There has to be an 'attention group' of sufficient size to ensure that the issue is heard and change occurs. The challenge is therefore not simply for individuals to broaden their approach to economics. It is for economists generally to be open to a wider range of approaches and to be more critical of the approaches that they use. This is harder, but the end result could be an exciting, vibrant, relevant discipline.

References

Dulleck U, Kerschbamer R (2006) On doctor, mechanics, and computer specialists: the economics of credence goods. J Econ Lit 44(1):5–42

Keynes JM (2007) The general theory of employment, interest, and money, New edn. Palgrave Macmillan, Basingstoke

Kurien CT (2012) Wealth and illfare: an expedition into real life economics. Books for Change, Bangalore

Marshall A (1920) Principles of economics. Retrieved from http://oll.libertyfund.org/title/1676

Smith A (2007) An inquiry into the nature and causes of the wealth of nations. Harriman House, Petersfield

Appendix

X_1 was 3 and heads, so Y_1 equals 3.

X_5 was 3 and tails, so contributes towards Y_6. X_6 was 6 and heads, so also contributes to Y_6, hence Y_6 equals 9.

Table A.1 Data for regression in Sect. 3.1.1

Obs. no.	Y	X	Obs. cont.	Y cont.	X cont.
1	3	3	26	5	4
2	0	2	27	0	3
3	2	5	28	6	3
4	5	1	29	0	1
5	1	3	30	6	5
6	9	6	31	6	6
7	0	6	32	1	1
8	7	1	33	0	3
9	1	1	34	3	5
10	5	5	35	5	2
11	2	2	36	2	3
12	2	2	37	8	5
13	0	4	38	0	4
14	10	6	39	9	5
15	0	1	40	3	3
16	7	6	41	0	1
17	0	6	42	5	4
18	9	3	43	1	1
19	0	1	44	0	1
20	7	6	45	1	1
21	3	3	46	1	1
22	0	1	47	5	4
23	3	2	48	1	1
24	1	1	49	0	3
25	0	1	50	9	6

S. Birks, *Rethinking Economics*, SpringerBriefs in Economics,
DOI 10.1007/978-981-287-176-3

Author Index

S. Birks, *Rethinking Economics*, SpringerBriefs in Economics,
DOI 10.1007/978-981-287-176-3

Subject Index

S. Birks, *Rethinking Economics*, SpringerBriefs in Economics,
DOI 10.1007/978-981-287-176-3

MIX
Papier aus verantwortungsvollen Quellen
Paper from responsible sources
FSC® C105338

If you have any concerns about our products,
you can contact us on
ProductSafety@springernature.com

In case Publisher is established outside the EU,
the EU authorized representative is:
Springer Nature Customer Service Center GmbH
Europaplatz 3, 69115 Heidelberg, Germany

Printed by Libri Plureos GmbH
in Hamburg, Germany